MISSOURI'S

Wicked
ROUTE 66

Gangsters and Outlaws on the Mother Road

....

Lisa Livingston-Martin

THE
History
PRESS

Published by The History Press
Charleston, SC 29403
www.historypress.net

Copyright © 2013 by Lisa Livingston-Martin
All rights reserved

Front cover: George Shepherd—fellow guerilla fighter, member of the James Gang and
would-be assassin of Jesse James. *Courtesy of the author.*
Back cover: William Lemp Jr. *Courtesy of the author.*

First published 2013

Manufactured in the United States

ISBN 978.1.60949.766.8

Library of Congress CIP data applied for.

For the Paranormal Science Lab team members.

Contents

Acknowledgements

I have been blessed by the support of many people during this project. I thank my family, who has put up with the demands on my time. My experiences with Paranormal Science Lab (PSL) have also been a large inspiration for this book. Follow PSL's research at www.paranormalsciencelab. com. Thank you to all of the Paranormal Science Lab team members, whose efforts made much of this project possible.

Paranormal Science Lab Team Members: Jordyn Cole, Mistie Cole, Eric Crinnian, Kelly Still Harris, Bill Martin, Carla Martin and Lisa Livingston-Martin.

Thank you to those who have been supportive of Paranormal Science Lab and its efforts to bring attention to and promote preservation efforts for historic sites such as the Kendrick House, the Olivia Apartments, the Galena Murder Bordello and the Burlingame and Chaffee Opera House. Thank you to Victorian Carthage, owner of the nonprofit Kendrick House. Thank you to Keith and Rachel McBride, owners of the Burlingame and Chaffee Opera House, and Mark Williams, owner of the Olivia Apartments. Thank you to the Joplin, Missouri Public Library; the Post Memorial Art Museum; Joplin, Missouri; and the Webb City, Missouri Library. Thank you to Danya Walker, Mike Harris, John Hacker, Joe Hadsall, Rebecca Haines, Kevin McClintock, Nikki Patrick, Leslie Simpson, Josh Shackles, the *Carthage Press*, the *Joplin Globe*, the *Pittsburg Morning Sun*, *Joplin Metro Magazine*, *Show Me the Ozarks* magazine, the Joplin Fuse, KOAM TV, KODE TV, KSN TV and the Missouri Humanities

Council for spreading the word. Thank you to all of those who have attended PSL activities, including the Haunted History Tours and live paranormal investigations at historic locations. We have made many new friends and enjoyed sharing history and the paranormal with the public.

I am indebted to the knowledge of many people in researching and writing this book. I want to thank Steve Cottrell, author and expert on history in southwest Missouri. I wish to extend a special thank-you to Janice Tremeear of Springfield, Missouri, and author of *Missouri's Haunted Route 66: Ghosts Along the Mother Road*, *Haunted Ozarks*, and *Wicked St. Louis* for encouragement and for the introduction to my editor, Ben Gibson. Special thanks to Ben Gibson and everyone at The History Press for making this book possible.

Chapter 1

Route 66

America's Road

Route 66 conjures some of the most nostalgic images of America: carefree adventure, vintage cars, roadside diners and kitsch motels. What "opened" in 1926 as Route 66 was built upon roads and trails that, in some places, had existed for centuries, evolving from Indian trails, settlers' routes and military roads. Just as Route 66 did not spring into existence in 1926 from a vacuum, the comforting images it now inspires do not tell the whole story of Route 66. The dark, wicked history of Route 66 tells an intriguing story of an America we often overlook. Route 66 started its westward trek in Chicago, Illinois, and passed through eight states before ending at the Pacific Ocean in California. Today, many retrace those 2,400-some-odd miles of asphalt and concrete on personal quests of discovery. The wicked secrets of Route 66 take a little more effort to be explored.

Travelers weren't alone on Route 66, and it didn't take long for the name to become associated with crime and violence. The 1920s exuded confidence and expansion of the economy. However, just three years after Route 66 opened, the Great Depression descended upon the nation, and the opportunities that had been so vibrant soon evaporated. These desperate times sent desperados upon America's road in the form of gangsters such as Bonnie and Clyde, the Ma Barker Gang and Pretty Boy Floyd. Missouri's section of Route 66 was familiar territory for Depression-era gangsters, but they weren't the first outlaws to frequent this road, nor would they be the last.

BULGER MOTOR CO.
520 W. Main, Carterville, MO 64835
(417) 673-1398

"On Route 66 Since 1946"

ROUTE
U S
66

Vintage postcard of the Bulger Motor Company in Carterville, Missouri, which opened on Route 66 in 1946 and is still in business, having survived the transition to the interstate highway system. *Courtesy of the author.*

By 1929, Missouri courts were forced to confront the issue of Route 66 being used to transport contraband. H.C. King was convicted of transporting moonshine. King lived along Route 66 in Crawford County in eastern Missouri. The sheriff raided King's home unsuccessfully, but sixteen miles down Route 66, King and his wife were found eating lunch at the Dew Drop Inn in Bourbon, Missouri. In the car were five one-gallon jugs of moonshine and a case of empty pint jars. The trial court, in convicting King, cited the statute that made transporting "moonshine," "hooch" or "corn whiskey" a felony. King appealed the conviction, relying on the testimony of a waiter at the Dew Drop Inn who stated that he had seen another car park beside King's car after King and his wife entered the diner. The waiter stated the driver was "monkeying" between the two cars, although he did not see the man put anything in King's car. The Missouri Supreme Court noted that the five gallons of whisky "in bulk" along with the case of empty pint bottles showed "preparations for some retailing operation." Nonetheless, in 1932, the court reversed the conviction, holding that there was not enough evidence to prove that King put the moonshine in his car or that he even knew it was there.

Although the form of contraband changed over the years, by 1994, Missouri courts routinely acknowledged it as a common practice when

Vintage postcard featuring the Chain of Rocks Bridge over the Mississippi, where Route 66 enters the state of Missouri in St. Louis. Tailfins are a symbol of the heyday of Route 66. *Courtesy of the author.*

upholding convictions for transporting illegal drugs. In the case of the *State v. Joyce* in 1994, the court noted:

> *Route 66 of legend and song no longer traverses Missouri. Now we have Interstate 44* [which follows much of the original Route 66], *on whose broad divided lanes thousands of vehicles cruise daily. Some of those vehicles transport controlled substances of various kinds, even to the point that courts may take judicial notice that this route is often used by traffickers.*

However, transporting contraband is far from the only less-than-reputable activity that has occurred along this famous route. As we explore the darker side of Route 66, we find that it does not tarnish the legend of America's Road but gives it facets little recounted. From Jesse James, Wild Bill Hickok and Belle Starr to Jack the Ripper and a mad scientist, Missouri's Route 66 has a wicked side that makes the legend even more fascinating.

Chapter 2

Jack the Ripper

St. Louis Connection?

Just as Route 66 makes its entrance into Missouri at St. Louis across the Chain of Rocks Bridge spanning the Mississippi River, Dr. Francis Tumblety flamboyantly swept into St. Louis as it fit his purposes, as murky as they seem in hindsight. Tumblety was the epitome of duplicity, a man living two lives. At best, he was a respected doctor living a personal life frowned upon by society, but at worst, he may have been the most infamous serial killer of all time.

Mystery shrouds Tumblety, although he lived much of his life very publicly. By different accounts, he was born in either Ireland or Canada in approximately 1833, no specific birth date being documented. Francis was the youngest of eleven children. The Tumblety family lived in Canada until they immigrated to the United States, where they settled in Rochester, New York. Francis Tumblety began practicing herbal medicine and became wealthy. He would move between cities such as Detroit, Boston, New York, D.C. and St. Louis, as well as traveling in Europe multiple times. At various times, Tumblety used aliases and ran afoul of the authorities. He was known for wearing "quasi-military" attire and claimed to have served as a surgeon for the Union army during the Civil War. He also claimed to be an acquaintance of Abraham Lincoln and other prominent officials.

Tumblety was suspected of treason and arrested in St. Louis in 1865 after apparently using the alias Blackburn and being mistaken as a notorious Confederate doctor of that name who had sent clothing infected with yellow fever from Bermuda to northern states. Tumblety was cleared of

Above: Vintage postcard featuring a night scene on the Mississippi in St. Louis. Notice the Eads Bridge, which was considered an engineering marvel upon its completion in 1874 as a combined railway and roadway. It was the longest arch-span bridge in the world at the time and was the first such bridge to use steel as the primary construction material. The riverboat *Admiral*, seen in the foreground, was built in 1907 as a paddle wheeler named the *Albatross* but was converted to its modern Art-Deco design in 1940. *Courtesy of the author.*

Right: Dr. Francis J. Tumblety, "Indian Herb Doctor" and Jack the Ripper suspect. Facsimile edition of October 1911 *St. Louis Globe-Democrat* published in 2001. *Courtesy of the author.*

Dr. Francis J. Tumblety
Is this man Jack the
Ripper? *Globe-Democrat File*

those allegations only to face other allegations that he had employed one of the conspirators who assisted John Wilkes Booth in the assassination of Abraham Lincoln. He was arrested for wearing a military uniform and impersonating a retired army surgeon in the St. Louis suburb of Carondelet in 1869. He was routinely observed in lavish attire riding a beautiful horse with a valet and greyhounds following behind. Tumblety seemed to seek attention through his public displays.

Tumblety went to extreme measures to maintain the image of a successful, distinguished doctor, even writing books of his life filled with purported testimonials from numerous prominent individuals and former patients. However, Tumblety's personal life threatened to ruin that reputation as much as his detractors. A young male protégé sued Tumblety for sexual assault, also asserting that Tumblety had warned him against women in general and prostitutes in particular. There were accounts that Tumblety and the young man were involved in a homosexual relationship. Many acquaintances later stated that they believed Tumblety did not like women and that he tended to avoid them. The source of this animosity toward women and prostitutes may stem from Tumblety's experiences as an abortionist. In 1857, while practicing in Montreal, Tumblety was arrested in connection with the death of a prostitute whom he had given drugs to terminate her pregnancy. Charges were not filed, but the incident forced him to leave town abruptly. Tumblety then went to St. John, New Brunswick, where in 1860, a patient, James Portmore, died after ingesting medicine prescribed by Tumblety. A coroner's inquest was convened, and Tumblety appeared before the assembled inquest. However, this time the outcome was a finding of medical negligence, and Tumblety fled the city.

In 1888, while on an extended tour of Europe, Tumblety was lodging in the Whitechapel district of London, the site of the Jack the Ripper murders. Why Tumblety, a wealthy American doctor, chose to stay in an impoverished area of London is unknown, although it seems likely that his personal behavior drew him to an area where he would not be recognized by members of London society. Tumblety was actually arrested in connection to the Ripper murders but released. Ten days later, Tumblety was arrested on eight counts of gross indecency and indecent assault with force and arms against four men from July to November 1888. Those charges were used at the time for prosecuting homosexual activity. Tumblety posted bail and, once again on the run, went to France before returning to New York. A Scotland Yard detective, Walter Andrews, followed Tumblety to the United States, and Tumblety responded by absconding from his apartment in New

Cartoon from the time of the Jack the Ripper murders portraying the police as being less than diligent in pursuing the perpetrator. Facsimile edition of October 1911 *St. Louis Globe-Democrat* published in 2001. *Courtesy of the author.*

York City. Another peculiar fact discovered about Tumblety was that he had a collection of human uteruses. Jack the Ripper removed the uterus from at least one of his victims. Tumblety disappeared for five years only to turn up again in St. Louis in 1893, where he remained until his death in 1903.

Was the flamboyant doctor Tumblety really Jack the Ripper? The question will likely never be resolved. Could Tumblety have realistically executed the murders? As a doctor with years of experience, he had both the knowledge and ability to proficiently dissect the bodies and remove internal organs, indignities suffered by the Ripper's victims. Then there was his unusual and morbid collection of human uteruses, also consistent with the removal of organs from Ripper victims. Tumblety also exhibited an irrational hatred of women, prostitutes in particular, whom the Ripper also targeted. Tumblety conspicuously took lodgings in Whitechapel, a very poor neighborhood, and thus had opportunity to commit the crimes. Perhaps even more difficult to explain is the doctor fleeing his apartment in New York when confronted by the Scotland Yard detective Andrews and remaining in hiding for five years. While one can argue that Tumblety had a long-standing pattern of fleeing the scene when attention was turned on his activities, he had not previously disappeared for such a long period of time. The doctor had instead shown a consistent pattern of quickly setting up shop in a new city, advertising and promoting claims of testimonials from famous people to solicit patients. The five-year hiatus may indicate a genuine fear of prosecution, or could be just one more unexpected move from an eccentric physician. However, five years of anonymity would not be the expected behavior from someone with this kind of extroverted, attention-craving personality.

Jack the Ripper and Francis Tumblety each left handwriting evidence. Interestingly, one Ripper letter listed a return address as "From Hell." Perhaps more than irony is responsible for the letter left in Philadelphia by Tumblety when he left town ahead of inquiries from the police, with a return address also listed as "From Hell." Michelle Dresbold and James Kwalwasser explored this physical evidence in their book *Sex, Lies and Handwriting*. After comparing handwriting characteristics in the two letters and finding a number of similarities, the authors make findings as to the personality of the writers. As for the author of the Jack the Ripper letter, Dresbold and Kwalwasser made the following comparisons with Francis Tumblety:

The writer was an extrovert.

Old acquaintances described how the self-promoting charlatan would call attention to himself after arriving in a new city by parading through the center of town, dressed in a medal-festooned uniform and followed by a valet and two greyhounds. As an energetic hustler who advertised heavily in local newspapers, Tumblety made a small fortune.

One New York acquaintance recalled that during the 1870s, Tumblety cordially invited any young men whom he fancied, wherever he met them, in the parks, squares or stores, to call upon him at this hotel, where he was wont to say he would show them an "easy road to fortune."

The writer had extreme sexual anger.

Tumblety was regarded as a misogynist. There are numerous accounts of Tumblety's "bitter hatred of women." A lawyer representing the mother of a young man Tumblety had once employed told a reporter: "I had a big batch of letters sent by him to the young man...and they were the most amusing farrago of illiterate nonsense. He never failed to warn his correspondents against lewd women, and in doing used the most shocking language."

Interestingly, many of Tumblety's patients were the very same lewd women he despised. [W]hen a young prostitute in Montreal died after an abortion in 1857, Tumblety was tried and acquitted. (A few years later, in St. John, New Brunswick, Tumblety was convicted of manslaughter. Tumblety jumped bail and fled to America before sentencing.)

Colonel C.A. Dunham, a prominent Washington attorney, reported that when Tumblety "was asked why he hated women, he said that when quite a young man he fell desperately in love with a pretty girl, rather his senior, who promised to reciprocate his affection. After a brief courtship he married her. The honeymoon was not over when he noticed a disposition on the part of his wife to flirt with other men. He remonstrated, she kissed him, called him a dear jealous fool—and he believed her. Happening to pass one day in a cab through the worst part of the town, he saw his wife and a man enter a gloomy looking house. Then he learned that before her marriage his wife had been an inmate [prostitute] of that and many similar houses. Then he gave up on all womankind."

Dunham also reported that Tumblety kept a collection of women's uteruses, in glass jars, which, he liked to brag, came from "every class of woman." It is believed that Tumblety acquired much of his collection as a result of botched abortions. The Whitechapel murderer cut out and took the uteruses of two of his victims, Annie Chapman and Kate Eddows.

The writer was violent.

Tumblety was arrested in London for "indecent assault with force and arms," which suggests he violently attacked his victims. Witnesses have described Tumblety's violent temper. In one incident, Tumblety was arrested for assaulting an editor in a New York hotel with a cane. Apparently, the editor had printed an article about Tumblety's murder trial in Canada a decade earlier.

The writer was semiliterate, with a rudimentary, grade-school education.

Tumblety attended only a few years of grade school.
"He was utterly devoid of education," said one childhood acquaintance from Rochester. "He lived with his brother, who was my uncle's gardener. The only training he ever had for the medical profession was a little drugstore at the back of the Arcade, which was kept by Dr. Lispernard, who carried on a medical business of a disreputable kind."

The writer had a chronic illness.

Hospital records indicate that Tumblety suffered from chronic nephritis and "valvular disease of the heart."

The writer was unkempt and had a nondescript, dirty appearance.

Clement R. Bennett, a well-known stenographer in the New York Circuit Court, met Tumblety in 1870, when he was impressed by Tumblety's "dash and hauteur." But when Bennett ran into Tumblety in 1879, he was then looking shabby, careworn, lame, appeared to be living a dissolute and dissipated life, and was begging for a night's lodging."

The writer was a liar or con artist.

Tumblety was a con artist who went by many aliases, including Frank Townsend, Frank Tumilty, Francis Twombelty, J.J. Blackburn, W.J. Morgan and Michael Sullivan. He lived his life as an imposter, pretending

"HE TURNED AND LOOKED AT ME."

Cartoon depicting a scene described by a possible witness of Jack the Ripper. Facsimile edition of October 1911 *St. Louis Globe-Democrat* published in 2001. *Courtesy of the author.*

to be an "Indian Herb Doctor," a decorated medical officer in the US Army, and a confidant of presidents, queens and emperors.

Tumblety reportedly made much of his money selling his bottled miracle cures, which he claimed were made from a combination of secret herbs and spices he learned from a Native American medicine man. In a number of cases, Tumblety's miracle cure turned out to be deadly. Tumblety's secret concoction of herbs, spices and alcohol was highly poisonous. This may explain the Herb Doctor's frequent changes of name and addresses.

After an extensive analysis comparing Tumblety's known handwriting to the Jack the Ripper letter, Dresbold and Kwalwasser make the following conclusion:

The handwriting in the "From Hell" letter matches Tumblety's bizarre personality trait by trait and matches Tumblety's bizarre handwriting stroke for stroke. And it proves, with a high degree of professional certainty, that Francis Tumblety was the cold-blooded killer known as Jack the Ripper.

To be sure, this is not a universal opinion held by Jack the Ripper experts, and there have been other old-standing suspects. Francis Tumblety spent his life carefully crafting a façade of respectability that was built upon eccentricity and shocking views and actions. Tumblety eluded capture despite a conviction for manslaughter and many other accusations while living very publicly for the majority of his life. It is not unthinkable that such a personality may have been an effective mask for the most infamous serial killer of all time.

Chapter 3

Joseph Nash McDowell

Brilliant Surgeon or Mad Scientist?

The very attributes that Francis Tumblety deeply craved—sophistication, education and respect in the medical profession—were found in abundance in Joseph Nash McDowell. Born into a prominent southern family and trained at Transylvania University in Lexington, Kentucky, McDowell was admired as the foremost expert on anatomy of his time, as well as an extraordinarily gifted surgeon. Also like Tumblety, McDowell was drawn to St. Louis early on, settling there in 1840 and joining the faculty of Kemper College. McDowell founded the medical school at Kemper College, later known as the Missouri Medical College and informally as McDowell's Medical College. McDowell's legacy lives on, as his medical college was the beginning of the distinguished Washington University in St. Louis Medical School. McDowell would serve as dean of the school until his death in 1868, except for his absence during the Civil War, during which he served in the Confederate army. McDowell saw St. Louis as an important city and central to the growth of his medical school, stating, "We believe the destiny of St. Louis in medicine is not to be equaled by any position in Western America."

Dr. McDowell was a striking figure, with a severe shock of flowing white hair, tall and thin with sculpted facial features, which together left an emaciated appearance. He also had a strong personality and was very demanding of his medical students, earning him the nickname "Sawbones." He also had strong animosities toward slaves and immigrants, although St. Louis was generally Northern in its convictions and home to many

Above: St. Louis developed into a major center of industry and commerce, which made it a natural choice for Route 66 to traverse. *Courtesy of the author.*

Right: Vintage postcard of the Missouri Medical College, better known as McDowell's Medical College. The college was built like a fortress and ultimately used as a military prison. *Courtesy of the author.*

thousands of immigrants, principally German and Irish. On the other hand, free medical care was provided to the city's poor. The college had a museum open to the public, with three thousand birds and animals from North America. Additional exhibits included minerals, fossils and antiquities. The public was welcome with an admission of twenty-five cents. However, clergy and "medical men" entered free of charge.

In his *Stanford University School of Medicine and the Predecessor Schools: An Historical Perspective*, John Wilson Long writes of McDowell:

> *As a lecturer in anatomy, he was truly gifted, with a marvelous power to entertain while driving home the subject. In the words of a student, he "made even the dry bones talk." He was wonderfully eloquent as a speaker and a master of extemporaneous invective, abuse and vilification when his ire was aroused, which was easily done. While a member of the medical faculty of Cincinnati College during Drake's campaign against the Medical College of Ohio, McDowell enthusiastically joined the fray by attacking the professors of the Ohio College openly in offensive language, vowing that given a year's time, he would blow the damned Ohio Medical College to hell. In St. Louis, he used similar tactics and exhibited a fanatical streak as well in his opposition to a rival medical school [St. Louis University]. His objectionable traits were at least partially, if not fully, offset by his devotion to family, friends and patients; by his consistently effective leadership of the medical school he founded; by his democratic relationship with students (frowned upon by his peers as unseemly fraternization); and by his ability as a surgeon, which was comparable to his proficiency in anatomy.*

Perhaps his political support of the Southern cause led to one of McDowell's most controversial acts, earning him a reputation of eccentricity. McDowell purchased more than 1,400 muskets and three small cannons (one reputedly having belonged to the French pirate LaFitte) in the late 1840s, ostensibly for purposes of sending them to Texas to fight to preserve Texas independence. For reasons unknown, the artillery remained in St. Louis and instead was stored in the medical college building. McDowell went to the trouble of installing the cannons in the tower of the octagonal medical school building at Eighth and Gratiot, barrels protruding from the windows, so that they were visible to passersby. In 1842, McDowell drew criticism with anti-Jesuit lectures. His derogatory remarks about Catholics came after the opening of the Medical College of St. Louis University, which then became a rival to his own medical school, and McDowell's termination as head physician at City Hospital by a Catholic mayor. Considered eccentric, he started wearing a breastplate and arming himself. He even mounted two of the three cannons aimed at Christian Brothers College, across the road.

Many Federal troops in St. Louis during the Civil War were German-American immigrants—targets of Dr. McDowell's outspoken comments. Reenactment photo. *Courtesy of the author.*

McDowell was not above defending his medical college from protestors through force of arms. Reenactment photo. *Courtesy of the author.*

Rumors of robbing graves to supply cadavers to the medical school as well as the medical school at nearby St. Louis University spread as their reputation for teaching anatomy grew. It is doubtful that any thought it necessary for McDowell to employ artillery in defense of the medical school, but the rumors of grave-robbing doctors coupled with the public's knowledge of McDowell's disdain of immigrants led to such necessity. Noted author and historian Charles van Ravenswaay, in his *St. Louis: An Informal History of the City and Its People, 1764–1865*, writes:

> *On February 25, 1844, some boys were playing ball on the commons near the medical department of St. Louis University (popularly known as Pope's College, after faculty member Charles Pope) on Washington Avenue near Eleventh St. The boys knocked their ball over the fence around the college yard. While searching for it, they stumbled upon an open vault which contained the remains of bodies from the dissection room. The boys ran off to report their discovery, and rumors began to spread about grave robbers. By mid-afternoon, a thousand people had gathered at the college threatening to destroy the building. By night, the crowd had tripled in size. The militia was ordered out, and the mayor urged the crowd to disperse. The mob broke up but later returned, broke into the building and destroyed furniture, equipment and specimens. Four years later, a German woman disappeared from her city home. The story spread that Dr. Joseph Nash McDowell, who had loudly damned "the Dutch," had lured her into the medical department of Kemper College and killed her for dissection. A mob gathered and began to throw stones against the building before making a general assault. But they underestimated Doctor McDowell. When the mob saw McDowell and some students loading and arming a cannon, they scattered in all directions. Two weeks later, the woman who had disappeared was found, demented, in Alton [Illinois].*

This was not the only time that McDowell had to fend off a mob at his medical college. Another time, a mob was protesting rumored grave-robbing activities at the school. The mob dispersed only when McDowell chased them away with his pet bear, which he kept at the medical school. McDowell wore breastplate armor to protect himself against harm from his enemies. The practice may have been prudent, for it is fairly clear that McDowell did associate with "resurrectionists," the euphemism of the day for grave robbers, buying the corpses for use at the medical school. By some accounts, McDowell and some of his students took a more direct approach to grave robbing, frequenting city cemeteries and retrieving corpses by moonlight.

McDowell appears to have had a long-standing belief in ghosts and, in fact, became a spiritualist, rejecting his Calvinistic upbringing. The following is taken from John Wilson Long's *Stanford University School of Medicine and the Predecessor Schools: An Historical Perspective*:

Anecdotes of McDowell's unconventional attitudes and behavior abound. He was either genuinely superstitious or, more likely, pretended to be. As an anatomist, he was often involved in the dangerous business of colluding with resurrectionists who provided his school with material for dissection. He told his cousin, the author Mary Ridenbaugh, of the following narrow escape which he ascribed to the intervention of his mother's spirit:

Said Cousin Mary, "I see that you listen to the spirits sometimes." "Yes," was Dr. McDowell's reply, "there is a great deal more in the matter than a man can express without being thought a d—n fool." "You are right," she added. "But have you ever had an experience or seen any manifestations?"

"Yes; confounded sight more than I tell people." "However," he continued, "I will tell you what I know and how I was saved by my mother's spirit."

"A German girl died with a very unusual disease, and we were determined to get her body for dissection. We got it and laid it in the college. The secret leaked out, and the Germans got their backs up and made things lively for us. [There was a large community of Germans in St. Louis.] *It was planned by them to come one night and hunt over the college to see if the body was there to be dissected. I received a note at my house at 9 o'clock of an evening warning me that the visit was to be that night."*

"I went down to the college about 11 o'clock, thinking to hide the corpse. When I got there, all was quiet. I went through the dissecting room, with a small lantern in my hand, in the direction of the body. I picked the cadaver up and threw it over my shoulder to carry it to the top loft to conceal it between the rafters or place it in a cedar chest that had stood in the closet for years."

"I had ascended one flight of stairs, when out went my lamp. I laid down the corpse and re-struck a light. I then picked up the body, when out went my light

again. I felt for another match in my pocket, when I distinctly saw my dear old mother standing a little distance off, beckoning to me. In the middle of the passage was a window; I saw her rise in front of it. I walked along close to the wall, with the corpse over my shoulder, and went to the top loft and hid it. I came down in the dark, for I knew the way well. As I reached the window in the passage, there were two Germans talking—one had a shotgun, the other a revolver. I kept close to the wall and slid down the stairs. When I got to the dissecting room door, I looked down the stairs into the hallway. There I saw five or six men lighting a lamp. I hesitated a moment as to what I should do, as I had left my pistols in my pocket in the dissecting room where I took the body. I looked in the room, as it was my only chance to get away, when I saw my spirit mother standing near the table from which I had just taken the corpse. I had no light, but the halo that surrounded my mother was sufficient to enable me to see the table quite plainly."

"I heard the men coming up the stairs. I laid down whence I had taken the body and pulled a cloth over my face to hide it. The men came in, all of them being armed, to look at the dead. They uncovered one body, it was that of a man, the next a man. Then they came to two women with black hair—the girl they were looking for had light flaxen hair. Then they passed me; one German said, 'Here is a fellow who died in his boots; I guess he is a fresh one.'

"I laid like marble. I thought I would jump up and frighten them, but I heard a voice, soft and low, close to my ear, say, 'Be still, be still.' The men went over the building and finally down stairs. I waited awhile, then slipped out. At the corner of Gratiot Street, I heard three men talking German. They took no notice of me, and I went home. Early in the morning, I went to the college and found everything all right. We dissected the body, buried the fragments and had no further trouble."

"Then, doctor, you feel satisfied that the spirit of your mother saved you from that trouble?"

"I know it," he replied. "I often feel as though my mother is near me when I have a difficult case of surgery. I am always successful when I feel this influence. Well, let me stop here. I have a boy to attend to with a broken leg, so goodbye." And with his characteristic manner of always being in a great hurry, he glided out the door and into his buggy.

McDowell also owned a cave outside of Hannibal, Missouri, known as McDowell's Cave. A small boy named Samuel Clemens, better known as Mark Twain, played in the cave. Later, it was reputed to serve as a hideout for Jesse James. In 1862, McDowell's Cave became the stage for a public experiment the likes of which had only previously been read about in Mary

Photograph of a very young newsboy in St. Louis, circa 1906. *Courtesy of the author.*

Shelley's *Frankenstein*. It also contributed to the perception that the doctor was insane. That year, when McDowell's fourteen-year-old daughter Anna died of pneumonia, he encased her body in an alcohol-filled copper tube and suspended it from the roof of the cave in an attempt to preserve it. The top was removable, and locals would often open the vault to look upon her face. This continued for two years until Hannibal officials convinced McDowell to move the body. It is believed that Anna was moved to the family mausoleum in St. Louis.

Mark Twain wrote McDowell Cave into *The Adventures of Tom Sawyer*, renaming it McDougall's Cave. He also included the character Dr. Robinson, who along with Injun Jim attempted to rob a grave, presumably to sell the body to a medical school. In the autobiographical *Life on the Mississippi*, Twain discusses the real-life McDowell Cave, including the story of Anna McDowell being preserved there. Later, due to the notoriety of the cave brought about by Twain's books, it was renamed Mark Twain Cave. In 1886, the cave was opened for tours, and it has been open to the public continuously since that time.

Joseph Nash McDowell recently received new notice in the best-selling book and movie *Abraham Lincoln: Vampire Hunter* as a corrupt doctor operating

Missouri was the scene of more than half of all Civil War battles during 1861 and more than all other states during the entire war except Virginia and Tennessee. Reenactment photo. *Courtesy of the author.*

a blood bank for vampires. In the novel, McDowell is put out of business by the vampire hunters but escapes to found his own medical school in St. Louis, where he installs cannons on the roof to ward off his attackers.

The McDowell Medical School has its own tale independent of the man for whom it was named. As McDowell left St. Louis for Memphis with his sons to enlist with the Confederate army, the city remained in Union hands, and the school building was confiscated. It was turned into a military prison and renamed the Gratiot Street Prison. It was rather unique in that large numbers of spies, guerrilla fighters and civilians imprisoned under General Order 11 (which authorized the arrest of any man who had not taken a loyalty oath to the federal government) were housed there. City residents were not immune to becoming prisoners either, as Thomas Goodrich writes:

> *Men are snatched off the streets and hurled into the dark prison cells of St. Louis and Jefferson City and never heard from again. Uncounted more were roused from sleep at night, dragged from their homes by Unionist death squads and murdered before the eyes of their horrified families.*

Vintage postcard of the King Brothers Motel in St. Louis, which was typical of the roadside motor lodges that dotted Route 66. *Courtesy of the author.*

Eventually, the three-story building held up to 1,300 prisoners, including female prisoners such as the famed Mayfield sisters, also known as the Lady Bushwackers of Vernon County, Missouri. Executions were carried out onsite, and the building suffered neglect during these years. After the war, McDowell returned and reopened the medical school. But by 1880, it was closed and empty. Today, the building is gone, and the parking lot for Ralston-Purina's corporate headquarters covers the area where the imposing medical school once stood.

Chapter 4

Lemp Family

Fortune and Tragedy

The tragedies that were to befall the Lemp family were not readily apparent. There were no public outbursts or eccentric behavior. Adam Lemp built a beer-brewing empire in St. Louis beginning in the 1840s. The Lemps were responsible for several milestones, including being first to transport beer by airplane. They made lager popular on a wide scale. They utilized massive caves under the brewery to store or lager beer, extending its shelf life. As their fortune grew, so too did the Lemp Mansion, including tunnels connecting the brewery to the house and a private theater and heated swimming pool in the cavern.

At its height, the Lemp Brewery was the third largest in the nation, and their signature beer, Falstaff, outsold Anheuser-Busch's Budweiser in St. Louis. Falstaff was distributed worldwide from London to Calcutta. The tide turned shortly after Adam's son William J. Lemp Sr. retired and turned over the management of the company to his sons. William Jr. "Billy," Frederick "Fred" and Charles were all highly qualified and accomplished. Continued success seemed assured for the Lemp family until Fred, his father's favorite, died of heart failure at the age of twenty-eight in 1901. Those close to William Sr. feared for his health as his grief deepened. He never recovered from the depression, and then, on January 1, 1904, Milwaukee brewer Frederick Pabst, his close friend and father-in-law of his daughter Hilda, passed away. Barely a month later, on February 3, 1904, William Sr. shot himself in the head in his bedroom in the Lemp Mansion. Billy Lemp took over duties as president of the brewery and

Claims Millionaire Brewer Allowed Boy 1

Lemp uses smiling women in its advertising to attract the attention of male customers. *Globe Files*

S;
lian
St. L
der I
show
be ¡
court
husb;
multi
have

S

tl

W

¡
an h
tion:
actu
toric
woi
I:
year
depc
solv
now
Geoi
the
Tum
Hos¡
Loui
""
per
time
iden
Two

Falstaff Beer was the signature brand of the William J. Lemp Brewery and outsold Anheuser-Busch's Budweiser in St. Louis. Facsimile edition of October 1911 *St. Louis Globe-Democrat* in published 2001. *Courtesy of the author.*

turned the family mansion into corporate offices. However, Billy was soon entwined in public scandal.

Billy had married Lillian Handlan, a belle of St. Louis society, in 1899, and the couple had one son. Lillian was known as the "Lavender Lady" due to her habit of exclusively wearing the color. Her obsession went deeper than her wardrobe, including having seven fine carriages all fitted in lavender upholstery and matching lavender harnesses. Billy filed for divorce in 1908, citing her obsession with the color as the basis for the separation.

The 1909 trial elicited a degree of voyeurism usually reserved for select murder trials, with all four of the St. Louis daily newspapers covering it in detail, prompting crowds to pack the courthouse for a glimpse of the drama as it unfolded in the courtroom. Billy also charged Lillian with drinking and smoking in public. Lillian countered with allegations of Billy's excessive drinking and adultery. The divorce was granted, and Lillian was awarded custody of their child, William III, "in large part based on the testimony of a servant who testified that she had found feminine hairs of various colors in William's bathroom while Mrs. Lemp was absent."

Not content to leave well enough alone, Billy and Lillian returned to court to argue about custody two years later, and the allegations grew to include violence. A family employee testified that "there had been a series of monkey and chicken fights at the Lemp brewery stables, and that young William III had witnessed live birds being fed to the monkeys." Lillian testified that Billy would threaten employees by taking his pistol out and conspicuously laying it on a table, and that Billy slaughtered neighborhood cats. Billy did not deny killing the cats but qualified his actions by saying that he did not kill cats for pleasure, only shooting those that disturbed his sleep.

Lillian was awarded sole custody of their only child and $6,000 in alimony per year. She then appealed to the Supreme Court, who awarded her a lump sum of alimony of $100,000—the largest such award in Missouri up to that time. Although Billy remarried a few years later, he and Lillian are buried in the mausoleum on either side of their son. As for Lillian, author Elizabeth Benoist said, "The Lavender Lady was pitiful after that. She still wore lavender, but she never got over the divorce."

The next suicide was that of Billy's sister Elsa, who had long suffered from depression. In 1919, she filed for divorce from her husband, Thomas Wright, and the court granted the divorce the same day. The couple remarried on March 8, 1920, but on March 19, 1920, she told her husband that she was having a bad night and wished to stay in bed the next morning. While Thomas took a bath, he heard a "sharp sound" and went to investigate.

Reproduction of a Lemp Brewing advertisement. *Courtesy of the author.*

Elsa had shot herself through the heart. Her brothers were called, and upon observing the scene, Billy said, "That's the Lemp family for you."

The next blow came with Prohibition. Billy was losing the will to run the business, and an attempt to convert to non-alcoholic beer was not successful. He simply closed the brewery without announcement, workers finding the doors locked as they reported for work.

The Lemps' fortunes continued to turn to tragedy. Author Carol Ferring Shepley writes:

Billy simply gave up. All of the owners of the plant were family members who did not always see eye to eye, and they were all independently wealthy. None of them had the mettle to make it through Prohibition. Moreover, Billy had never modernized operations; he clung to traditional methods. On June 28, 1922, the buildings were sold at auction, mostly to International Shoe Company. Three years before, they had been estimated to be worth $7 million, but they sold for $585,000.

Despondent over having to dismantle his family's business, Billy grew increasingly depressed. On December 29, 1922, putting a revolver to his chest, he shot himself through the heart in his office in the mansion where his father had committed suicide. Like his father and sister, he left no suicide note. Within minutes, his son, William J. Lemp III, was kneeling over his body, crying, "I was afraid this was coming." Two days later, the funeral was held in the company offices where William Sr.'s services had taken place eighteen years earlier.

William III attempted unsuccessfully to revive Lemp beer after the repeal of Prohibition in 1933, even though Falstaff and the Lemp shield had been sold to Joe Griesedieck, who was making a go of it. In 1939, William entered into an agreement with Central Breweries of East St. Louis, Illinois, which changed its name to William J. Lemp Brewing Company. While initial sales figures looked good, a year and a half later, the company went bankrupt. William III dropped dead of a heart attack at age forty-three in 1943. Charles Lemp, Billy's brother, was the fourth family suicide. While he had been treasurer and later vice-president of the brewery, he withdrew from the family business and went into banking. In 1911, he moved out of the family mansion and into the Racquet Club. In 1929, still unmarried, he moved back into the Lemp mansion. He became increasingly reclusive, arthritic, and ill. At age seventy-seven, he too took his life. On May 10, 1949, he lay down in bed and put a bullet through his head. He was the only Lemp to leave a suicide note, which read: "In case I am found dead, blame it on no one but me." He had prepaid for his funeral and requested that his ashes be buried at his farm.

Today, the Lemp Brewery stands mostly empty, and the caverns have been neglected, with many passages left impassable. The mansion fell upon hard times as well. Shortly after Charles's death, it was turned into a boardinghouse. By the 1970s, it was in poor condition but was purchased by private parties, renovated and reopened as a restaurant. Stories of

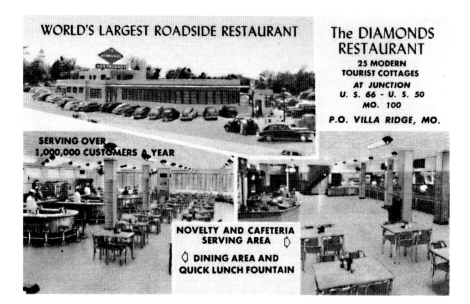

The Diamonds Restaurant in Villa Ridge, Missouri, claimed to be the largest roadside eatery in the world. *Courtesy of the author.*

hauntings started soon after Charles's death. In 1980, *Life* magazine named the mansion as one of the nine most haunted houses in America.

Perhaps the most tragic story to come from this tortured family is that of Zeke, the youngest child of William Lemp Sr. and his wife, Julia. Zeke was born with physical deformities and mental deficits. There is no birth certificate, and it is speculated that the parents would have been pressured to institutionalize the child. Instead, he was raised in the home, and after his parents died, Billy took over responsibility for his youngest brother. The Lemp Mansion website tells the story of Zeke:

> *Folklore states Zeke was locked in the attic...this is untrue. Back then, the attic served as the servants' quarters. The servants loved Zeke and doted upon him, and the attic served as a safe place for him to play, as he had the constant attention of the Lemp staff and an outdoor patio high above the jeers from neighborhood children. Zeke died at the age of sixteen as a result of falling down the servants' stairs.*

You can visit the Lemp Mansion as you travel Route 66 from St. Louis west across Missouri, and you may well run into one of the Lemp family members still walking the halls of the mansion.

Chapter 5

Devil's Elbow

Murder Unpunished

The town of Devil's Elbow, Missouri, takes its name from a feature of the Big Piney River. The images conjured by the name imply an atmosphere of mystery and intrigue. The town, which enjoyed the advantage of being situated on Route 66 before the days of the interstate, is located in Pulaski County, not far from Rolla and Waynesville. Mystery is not far away either. Two miles outside of town is a gravel road leading to the often-overgrown Mayfield Cemetery. Alongside the gravel road is the gravesite of Eliza Jane Laycocks Thomas. There is no explanation as to why this lonely grave sits beside the gravel road. Census records show that Eliza was fifteen years old in 1880 and living with her parents in Phelps County,

just a few miles away. The grave marker lists a death date of 1897 and that she was the wife of Henry Thomas. No information was found about Henry Thomas, and this isolated grave poses a mystery over one hundred years later—a story forever lost to time. There are other similar stories of unmarked graves of Irish workmen who

Route 66 became a symbol of freedom as Americans took to the highways to explore the country. This vintage photograph was taken near Lebanon, Missouri. *Courtesy of the author.*

died in the area, but the worst story of death in this small area involves a murderer who has remained unpunished for over forty years.

Three young men working at the Soto Service Club at the nearby Fort Leonard Wood army base were kidnapped during a robbery wherein approximately $3,600 was taken from the safe. The men, who ranged in ages from eighteen to thirty-two, were forced into a car, driven to Devil's Elbow and then ordered to lie face down in the woods just off the road. All three were shot in the back of the head. The indictment read in part:

> *On or about the 18th day of October, 1968, at Fort Leonard Wood, in the Western District of Missouri, on land acquired for the use of the United States and under the exclusive jurisdiction thereof, Major Becton and Harry Dino Word, aka Harry Dino Hurd, did then and there willfully, unlawfully, and feloniously make an assault in and upon one Wayne Eugene Gilbert, Harold Joe Presley, and Bobby Dean Tryan, with a dangerous and deadly weapon, to wit, a gun which was loaded with gun powder and leaden balls, and did feloniously rob, steal, take and carry away certain property, to wit, money in the aggregate value of $3,636.95, the money being the personal property of the Soto Service Club, and the said Wayne Eugene Gilbert, Harold Joe Presley and Bobby Dean Tryan, who had custody of property stolen from the person and against the will of the said Wayne Eugene Gilbert, Harold Joe Presley, and Bobby Dean Tryan, then and there by force and violence to the person of the said Wayne Eugene Gilbert, Harold Joe Presley and Bobby Dean Tryan.*

Hurd was arrested and convicted in connection with the robbery and murders, receiving a life sentence. But on appeal, the Federal Court of Appeals determined that he had been sentenced under the wrong statute and could only be sentenced to fifteen years for the robbery, deferring to the prosecutor of Pulaski County to file murder charges. On July 7, 1977, Hurd filed a motion for a new trial in view of newly discovered evidence. Judge Collinson denied that motion on February 3, 1978. Hurd filed another motion on March 9, 1978, stating that he had been denied effective assistance of trial counsel. A hearing on this motion was held on August 30, 1978. At the hearing, Hurd testified about his attorney's conduct of the trial and produced three witnesses his trial attorney had allegedly failed to subpoena or interview: Rachel York, one of his beauty shop customers; Charles Bratton, an acquaintance; and Mrs. Ethel Hurd, his mother.

Vintage postcard of the Devil's Elbow Café. Although the roof is absent, the vintage gas pumps still stand, giving the scene an eerie effect. *Courtesy of the author.*

York testified that Hurd had styled her hair on the night of the robbery. When asked how she could remember that night, York said that it was the Friday night following her miscarriage, which had occurred on October 12 or 13. The following Friday was October 18, the date of the robbery. The U.S. attorney had not been aware of the alibi prior to the witness's testimony. After the hearing, he contacted the hospital at Fort Leonard Wood and requested a copy of York's medical records relating to the miscarriage. The hospital staff said that the records were held in a regional office in St. Louis. After receiving the records from the regional office, the attorney discovered that the miscarriage had occurred on October 9, placing York, by her testimony, in Hurd's beauty shop on October 11, a week before the robbery. Judge Collinson allowed the prosecution to submit York's hospital records by motion on October 6, 1978. Bratton testified that two men involved in the robbery had divided the loot at his home and discussed the robbery without mentioning Hurd. Mrs. Hurd stated that she had seen her son and York at the beauty shop at the time of the robbery.

Hurd's conviction was upheld. However, neither Hurd nor the other suspect, his brother Chester Hurd, were tried for murder. Chester was found dead a few years later, an apparent suicide by hanging. Dino Hurd has not

The Greyhound bus station, another symbol of travel and mobility along Route 66. *Courtesy of the author.*

been sighted since his release from prison, although there is speculation that he is living in another state under an assumed name. Local residents haven't forgotten what happened here so many years ago. There has been inquiry about pursuing the murder charges, and residents still wait for a murderer to receive punishment.

Chapter 6

The Wild West Gunfight Is Born on Route 66

While Route 66 was given its name in Springfield, Missouri, in 1926, sixty-one years earlier, the legend of the Wild West shootout was born on the square in Springfield. Although Springfield was more Southern in its sympathies at the outset of the Civil War, it served as Union headquarters from the time of the Battle of Carthage (July 5, 1861) until the Confederate victory at the Battle of Wilson's Creek (August 10, 1861), which occurred just miles outside of Springfield. As for the southwest portion of the state, the Confederates were in full control and remained so until their defeat at Pea Ridge, Arkansas, in 1862.

Downtown Springfield is filled with Civil War sites. The old courthouse on the square was used as a military hospital for four years, and wounded from the Battles of Carthage and Wilson's Creek were treated there. The square would also be the scene of one of the most iconic gunfights in America, arising out of tensions of two soldiers—one Union and one Confederate—over a dispute in a card game. James Butler Hickok, better known as "Wild Bill" Hickok, was a Union scout and spy who, prior to the outbreak of the war, had served the army in Bloody Kansas, defending the slaveholding settlers there from violence of the abolitionists, exemplified by Jim Lane's Redlegs and John Brown's retaliatory massacres in eastern Kansas and extreme western Missouri.

For many men who fought in this region, friendships often transcended politics. After the end of hostilities in the spring of 1865, Hickok remained in Springfield, Missouri, spending much of his time at poker tables. He became

Above: The Civil War was the firestorm in which the Old West was born, for both lawmen and outlaws. Reenactment photo. *Courtesy of the author.*

Left: James Butler Hickok, better known as "Wild Bill," was an army scout during the Civil War. At the age of twenty-nine, he became a celebrated gunslinger, participating in the only documented gunfight of the Wild West wherein the participants lined up and shot at each other. *Courtesy of the author.*

friends with Dave Tutt, a former Confederate soldier, but that friendship turned deadly in July 1865, when an argument erupted between the two over allegations of cheating at cards. The argument led to one of the most infamous gunfights in American history, one that resembled the iconic images of Hollywood—two gunfighters facing off one-on-one out in the open. The two met on the square, which in many respects appears much the same as it did then: an open interior square framed by streets and buildings. On the northwest corner stood the Greene County Courthouse, which had seen direct service in the Civil War as the general hospital for the Union army. Tutt stood in front of the courthouse, while

Civil War soldiers, even those who fought on opposite sides, often became close friends after the war. Tutt was a Confederate, while Hickok was a Union army scout. Reenactment photo. *Courtesy of the author.*

Hickok stood on the southeast corner of the square. Hickok shot Tutt, who turned, staggered toward the courthouse steps and exclaimed "I'm dead, boys" before hitting the ground.

The events were covered in *Harper's Weekly*, propelling Hickok to fame. The shootout also led to Hickok being tried for murder. The trial is reenacted for the public periodically and provides a glimpse into early justice in the American West. More than twenty witnesses present on the square at the time of the gunfight were called to testify, but only four admitted to actually seeing any of the fight firsthand. Even at that, some claimed they did not see Hickok pull the trigger. It was unclear whether Tutt had gotten off a shot before he was hit, as one witness stated that he had heard only one shot, even though he could see neither of the men.

Above: Print depicting the Hickok-Tutt gunfight. First-hand accounts state that Hickok walked onto the square in Springfield with a rifle and not a pistol as shown. Artist Andy Thomas. *Courtesy of the author.*

Left: Reproduction of a drawing depicting Hickok confronting Tutt on the square in Springfield. The men were actually facing each other on diagonal corners. *Courtesy of the author.*

Perhaps out of frontier practicality, Hickok was acquitted of all charges, despite the fact that he had walked onto the square with a loaded rifle with the announced intent of engaging in a gunfight with Tutt. This would not be the last infamous gunfight in the area.

Perhaps it should not be surprising that the high-noon showdown was born in Springfield, as the city's first murder occurred in a similar fashion.

The killer was Judge Charles S. Yancey, of the county court. Yancey had fined the man he later killed, John Roberts, for a misdemeanor, and Roberts had threatened his life for so doing. On May 28, 1837, Roberts attacked Yancey on the square, but the judge drew his pistol and shot Roberts dead. This was the same location where the Hickok-Tutt gunfight would occur twenty-eight years later. A trial was held, and like Hickok, Yancey was acquitted on the plea of self-defense.

Chapter 7

The Young Brothers

Largest Massacre of Law Enforcement in American History Before 9/11

While many Depression-era gangsters who drove Route 66 became famous, the largest shootout with police involves names largely lost to history, despite the fact that they were responsible for killing more law enforcement officers in any incident in American history until the events of September 11, 2001.

Two of eleven children of J.D. Young and his wife, Willie, brothers Jennings and Harry Young were not typical criminals. The family resided in the small community of Brookline, just southeast of Springfield, Missouri, and enjoyed the quiet life on the farm. But all that would change on January 2, 1932.

Trouble had been brewing for several years. Jennings and brother Paul were arrested in 1918, charged with robbing stores owned by friends and neighbors. Their father was a respected citizen and was allowed to bond out his sons without putting up any property. The sons were convicted and remanded to the state penitentiary for a total of ten years. J.D. died in 1921, and within three years, criminal charges were filed against several of the sons and their mother (as an accomplice) after they were caught breaking into a freight car on a train and stealing merchandise. Jennings pled guilty, and the other defendants were never tried. Younger brother Harry soon started his criminal career with the minor offense of altering the ID number on a motor in a car, followed by robbery, for which he was sentenced to the Missouri State Penitentiary. During his stay in the "big house" in Jefferson City, Harry met "Pretty Boy" Floyd, who was also serving time for robbery.

The Young farmhouse as depicted by police following the "massacre." Taken from John R. Woodside's *The Young Brothers Massacre* (1932), written and illustrated especially for law enforcement officers. *Courtesy of http://www.chrisanddavid.com.*

After the massacre, Floyd visited the Young family multiple times, checking in on the sisters and mother. In 1929, Harry was involved in the shooting of Mark Noe, a police officer in nearby Republic, Missouri. Willie would say later that in the more than two years between Noe's death and the massacre, she had seen Harry only two times.

On December 30, 1931, Harry and Jennings showed up at the family farm unannounced and spent the next few days trying to sell the stolen car they were driving. But a dealer in Springfield tipped off police when he suspected that the car was stolen. The brothers had enlisted two of their sisters, Lorena and Vinita, to unwittingly sell the car for them. While being questioned by police, the sisters eventually admitted that Harry and Jennings were at the farm. Officers went to the farm, where they arrested Willie and brought her back to Springfield. On January 2, 1932, ten officers set out in three cars to arrest the Young brothers at the farmhouse in Brookline. But the officers had not planned the arrest, and upon arriving and finding a locked door, they stood discussing their options. Just minutes after their arrival, six officers had been shot dead and three wounded. Harry and Jennings Young made their escape by car, and a crowd began gathering around the house. Demands to torch the house escalated, and some dragged a mattress onto the porch and

WANTED

$1,000 REWARD

Will be paid to any person or person(s) with information leading to the arrest (DEAD or ALIVE) of:

L. L. ALERT

F. B. L. A

George R. Kelly, a.k.a., "Machine Gun" Kelly

CRIMES

George "Machine Gun" Kelly is being sought on a variety of charges including bootlegging, armed robbery, & kidnapping of wealthy Oklahoma City resident Charles F. Urschel & his friend, Walter R. Jarrett in July 1933.

Description

Place of Birth: Memphis, Tn. Birthdate: July 18, 1895 Height: 5' 9 ½" Weight: 172 lbs. Hair:

Caution

Kelly is an 'Expert Machine Gunner' and is known to be armed at all times with a Thompson .45 caliber sub machine gun, presented to him by his wife, Geneva Ramsey, also being sought as a material witness.

Remarks

Reproduction of a wanted poster for George "Machine Gun" Kelly, bootlegger, bank robber and one of many Depression-era gangsters and outlaws who traveled Route 66 on crime sprees. *Courtesy of the author.*

48

set it on fire. Officers trying to convince the mob that burning the house would destroy evidence had to stomp out the flames. The house had been shot full of holes and ransacked. Willie and her daughters were eventually released, but their home had been destroyed.

Three days later, on January 5, 1932, after what has been called the largest manhunt in Texas history, Houston police descended upon the house where Harry had been living under an assumed name. They stormed the house to find that the two brothers had entered into a suicide pact, each one shooting the other as the police came through the door. Jennings was also hit by a shotgun blast from one of the officers. Ironically, the file on the incident has disappeared from the records of the Houston police department. The rest of the Young family went about rebuilding their lives.

Chapter 8

Mob Violence and Lynching

Racial tensions carried over from the Civil War and broke out in several places in southern Missouri in the late 1800s and early 1900s. Both Springfield and Pierce City were sites of lynchings. The case of the lynching of Thomas Gilyard in Joplin, Missouri, demonstrates the volatility of the situation. The feelings from the Civil War that led to the mutilation of bodies of black soldiers at the Rader Farm Massacre near Joplin flared again almost exactly forty years later.

The population of African Americans increased as the general population swelled in the new mining town. In 1880, there were 7,038 total residents, and of those, 246 were African American. By 1910, Joplin's population was 26,023, with 773 being African American. Mining was segregated in the area, and virtually no Negroes worked in the mines. Other well-paying industries were segregated as well. On April 2, 1903, the Freeman Foundry faced a worker strike because seventy white workers protested J.W. Freeman hiring Sidney Martin, a black man. A spokesman for the workers told the *Joplin Globe*, "While they would not raise such strenuous objections to the one colored man, they believe that if one is allowed to work here it will be but a short time until more are employed, and they want it understood right in the beginning that colored men are not wanted." To avoid a strike, Freeman relented and let Martin go. As a consequence, blacks generally worked in service jobs or performed unskilled labor.

A byproduct of the mining industry was that miners tended to compensate for the rough work by spending much of their paychecks in the many saloons in town. Violence often accompanied the flow of alcohol. Such was the case on April 16, 1903, when a mob lynched a young black man, Thomas Gilyard, on the streets of Joplin. It was not the first time the citizens had resorted to lynching. In 1885, a mob lynched a white man, Joe Thornton, who had killed police officer Daniel Sheehan. Just three years earlier, a mob tried to lynch Leonard Barnett, a black man who was accused of raping a white girl, but he was moved out of town before the mob could accomplish its goal.

The previous day, hardware merchant Sam Bullock had reported to the police that he had two pistols stolen from his store and suspected that two "colored men" were the culprits. A black man who said he knew where these men were now located accompanied Bullock to the police station. Shortly thereafter, the two men and Officer Ben May headed to the Kansas City Southern rail yards in north Joplin, where the witness said the thieves were hiding. Soon, Officer Theodore Leslie was sent to join the search. Leslie approached a black man standing inside a stock car and patted him

Police officers posing for a portrait, circa 1890s. Upon close inspection, a map of Missouri can be seen hanging on the wall behind the men. *Courtesy of the author.*

down. Gunshots rang out from within the railcar, and Leslie returned fire. However, Leslie fell to the ground mortally wounded, having been hit in the chest and through the eye. Bystanders who witnessed the gunfire chased the black man as he fled on foot, and seventeen year-old Ike Clark fired his gun at the assailant and wounded him, but the black man escaped. An all-out manhunt ensued, and police officers from nearby towns soon joined the pursuit. The *Joplin Globe* offered a $100 reward for the capture of the killer, and the reward soon grew to $1,650. The next day, two workers at the Bauer Brothers slaughterhouse apprehended the suspected killer after they wrestled the man's gun from him. As the two men took the suspect to the police station, he admitted to them that he had been in the railcar when Leslie was shot but that there were three other men in there and that he did not fire at the officer.

Once at the jail, a crowd started to gather, demanding immediate punishment. As a precaution, the saloons were ordered closed for two hours, but this just meant that angry men had nowhere to congregate, and the crowd outside the jail grew even larger. Someone in the crowd yelled, "Break the jail down!" and several men appeared with a ten-foot-long battering ram and started pummeling the brick wall of the jail. Police officers confiscated the battering ram, but it was soon replaced by another. After ten minutes, the mob had breached the jail wall. The mob busted the lock on Gilyard's cell door with a sledgehammer and dragged him outside into the street. The jail stood on the southeast corner of Joplin Avenue and Second Street, which is now a parking lot. The mob, now numbering an estimated three thousand men, women and children, dragged Gilyard down the street to Wall and Second Street to the present-day site of the Greyhound bus station. Several city officials had tried to stop the mob before it broke into the jail to no avail. As the mob was trying to throw a rope over a cross arm of a telephone pole, Perl Decker, the city attorney, rode through the crowd on horseback. He had Ike Clark, the seventeen-year-old who had chased and wounded Officer Leslie's murderer, on the horse with him. Clark yelled to the crowd that Gilyard was not the man he shot and that he definitely wasn't the man he saw kill Officer Leslie. The rope was now around Gilyard's neck. Dr. Jesse May attempted to cut the rope with his knife while men in the mob hoisted Gilyard aloft with the other end of the rope. Mayor Trigg and Mayor-elect Tom Cunningham also tried to cut the rope until they were forced at gunpoint to stop. A few other unnamed men tried to pull the rope back to keep Gilyard from being hoisted off his feet.

Few driving down Route 66 would have suspected that streets along their way had been the sites of mob violence and lynchings. Reenactment photo. *Courtesy of the author.*

The *Joplin Daily News Herald* reported that Gilyard cried out, "Oh, God don't!" He continued to plead with the mob, "Lord God knows dat I am innocent. Gemmen, I's got a father an' a mother. Please, foah de luhb o' massey, send foah my poor old mother before you kill me." But the men trying to stop the lynching were "savagely" driven off, and Gilyard was hoisted aloft. The *Herald* reported, "A metal spike on the pole hit Gilyard's head, but he did not respond if he felt any pain. His eyes closed, his jaw fell slack. Thomas Gilyard was dead." It was 5:50 p.m.

By 8:00 p.m., a group of men had gathered and began marching up Main Street demanding that all blacks leave Joplin. The police were unable to disperse the crowd. City officials appealed to businesses and citizens to intervene, but again to no avail. The crowd then focused on businesses that employed blacks, first targeting the Imperial Barbershop, which employed black men as barbers. Police officer Ben May was able to slow the crowd and allow the black barbers time to escape out the back. The crowd was disappointed to find no blacks inside and moved on to begin a new round of violence. A white man, "Hickory Bill," was arrested for disturbing the peace and firing his gun and was taken to the jail. When the mob realized this had happened, they once again marched on the jail, demanding that

Hickory Bill be released. The police refused to meet their demand, and the mob then threatened to blow up the jail with dynamite. After a standoff, the police realized that they were outnumbered and the mob would not be dissuaded, so they released Hickory Bill. But according to Kimberly Harper in *White Man's Heaven: The Lynching and Expulsion of Blacks in the Southern Ozarks, 1894–1909*, this did not calm the mob:

The angry mob continued to grow in size as it roamed Joplin's downtown. Between Broadway and A Streets, the mob threw rocks and other objects "at houses, through windows and at fleeing negroes." The aim of the crowd was apparently good, as a reporter observed, "There is scarcely a whole window pane in a window" on either street. The crowd managed to overturn one house before it moved on. The mob fired pistols into the air as it boldly paraded unchallenged in the night air. The boisterous crowd provided adequate warning of their approach as they thundered, "White folks get in line." They also warned, "White folks keep your lights burning." The crack of rifles and bursts of pistol fire were accompanied by the sound of glass breaking. Curiously, a quartet of young men followed the mob, singing songs that lightened the mood.

The horde of rioters swept past Fifth and Main Streets, headed for the black section of town located at the north end of Main Street. The area had previously been inhabited by "lewd" women who were driven out by a mob just months earlier. After the prostitutes were chased out, black families moved in, including several from Pierce City [where lynchings of blacks had also recently occurred]. *Some of Joplin's black residents had already fled earlier that day. The blacks who were chased from Pierce City undoubtedly knew they were about to be caught up in another explosion of racial violence. They wisely fled before the mob called on them. Callers from Webb City and Galena phoned to let Joplin officials know that both cities had been inundated by a flood of black refugees "as soon as possible after the mob began to form to hang the murderer of Theodore Leslie."*

Bob Carter was one of the first to leave shortly after the lynching. Carter told a reporter he left because the lynching brought back "disagreeable memories" of a time when "owing to a little unpleasantness some citizens of Granby [Missouri] *forced him to stretch a new rope for several minutes about two years ago. The mob torched six homes. The mob returned to East Seventh Street, another black area in Joplin, and set more houses on fire. At one of the fires, the firemen were unable to do much good. As fast as a line of hose was strung, the mob stuck knives in it. As the mob ran rampant, though, Joplin's streets filled with blacks too scared to wait on trains to take them to safety. Ike Beechum, a black resident of Carthage, told [a] reporter that his nephew was among those who fled Joplin at the last minute. When asked if his nephew arrived in Carthage by train from Joplin, Beechum replied, "Lord, no. He beat the cars—he came over on foot."*

To the city's credit, even as the mob was vandalizing homes and setting fires, five hundred volunteers were quickly assembled to prevent further mob violence. A coroner's inquest was called two days later, and Gilyard's body was examined. It was determined that a gunshot to the leg had entered from below and lodged near his spine. This was consistent with Officer Leslie shooting at someone above him standing inside the rail car. Ike Clark changed his story and testified that he believed Gilyard was the man he chased after Leslie was killed. Gilyard, it turned out, was a transient from Mississippi hopping the rail on his way to Asbury, Missouri, to join a railroad work gang. Three men were arrested for the lynching, including Hickory Bill. Sam Mitchell, one of the men charged in connection with the lynching, was identified as the man who secured the rope and climbed the telephone pole to throw it over the cross arm. He was convicted by an all-white jury

While the mob roams Joplin's streets looking for more victims, citizens organize to bring the mob to justice. Reenactment photo. *Courtesy of the author.*

and sentenced to ten years in prison. A new trial was granted based on motions filed by his attorney after the trial. In the second trial, the jury flinched and did not convict him. There is speculation that the reason for the jury acquitting him was that should he be convicted, potentially every man, woman and child in that mob would be held responsible. The court records for Hickory Bill and the third defendant have been lost, but it appears that they were not convicted or possibly that the charges were dismissed after Mitchell was acquitted.

Chapter 9

Bonnie and Clyde

A Legend Is Born on Route 66

The Great Depression spawned numerous bank robbers and criminals born of the desperate economic conditions, and then the Dust Bowl imposed even more harsh conditions on the Midwest. Bank robberies during this time period were concentrated in the Midwest, with a disproportionate share occurring in Oklahoma. Many of the gangsters, bank robbers and other fugitives found their way through Joplin during this time. Herbert Allen "Deafy" Farmer grew up in Webb City, Missouri, and was a childhood acquaintance of Ma Barker and her sons, as the Barker family lived in Webb City until 1915 before moving to Tulsa, Oklahoma. The two families maintained their friendship through the years, and during the Great Depression, Herbert Farmer and his wife, Esther, ran a safe house for gangs in Joplin. The FBI summary on Ma Barker's Karpis-Barker gang concluded that the Barker boys had been taught their skills in crime by Herbert Farmer. The Farmers were involved in the planning of the infamous Kansas City Massacre, during which four policemen were killed, along with Jelly Nash, who had escaped from Leavenworth Prison but had been captured and was at the Union Station with federal agents returning him to Leavenworth.

Although the Barkers gave Farmer $2,500 to live on during the aftermath of the Kansas City Massacre, Farmer made statements to police during his interrogation suggesting that the Barkers were involved in the Union Station shootings, although they were not involved. In 1934, Farmer was convicted of conspiracy to aid a federal prisoner's escape in connection with Jelly Nash and sentenced to the maximum sentence: two

$1,200.00 REWARD $1,200.00

Twelve Hundred Dollars.

WANTED

For the Murder of C. R. Kelly, Sheriff of Howell County, Missouri, on December 19, 1931

Members of the **Karpis/Barker** gang of Texas, Oklahoma, Missouri & Kansas

Kate *"Ma"* Barker   Arthur *"Doc"* Barker   Fred Barker   Alvin *"Creepy"* Karpis

Alvin *"Creepy"* Karpis, alias George Dunn, alias R. E. Hamilton, Ray Karpis, & Raymond Hadley; Age 22, Height 5' 9", Weight 133 lbs., Hair Brown, Eyes, Blue. Occupation worked in bakery.

Fred Barker, Age 28, Height 5' 4", Weight 120 lbs, Complexion fair.

Arthur *"Doc"* Barker; Age 25, Height 5' 6", Weight 128 lbs., Hair black, Eyes brown, Complexion ruddy.

Kate *"Ma"* Barker, Age 50's, Height 5' 3", Weight 165(est.), Hair dyed black, Eyes brown.

These individuals acting together *Murdered* Sheriff C. R. Kelly, West Plains, Missouri, in *"cold blood"* when he attempted to arrest them.

The **Chief** of Police and Sheriff at West Plains, Missouri, will pay a reward of **$300.00** each for the arrest and surrender of either of these persons to **Howell County, Missouri,** officers. This jurisdiction holds *Felony Warrants* on all of the above named individuals for the crime of *Murder.*

Police & other authorities: Keep this Poster before you at all times as we want these Fugitives. If further information is needed, Wire Collect Sheriff of West Plains.

James A. Bridges
Chief of Police

Mrs. C. R. Kelly
Sheriff

West Plains, Missouri

Reproduction of a wanted poster for the Ma Barker Gang (also known as the Karpis-Barker Gang) issued by the West Plains Police Department and the Howell County Sheriff's Department for the killing of Sheriff C.R. Kelly on December 19, 1931. *Courtesy of the author.*

years in prison and a $10,000 fine. Esther Farmer was given probation and assessed a $5,000 fine. Herbert Farmer served his sentence in Leavenworth before being transferred to the new federal prison at Alcatraz. After his release, he returned to Joplin, where he and Esther lived until his death in 1948. Later, Esther married Harvey Bailey, known as the "dean of the American bank robbers." They remained in Joplin the rest of their lives. Bailey died in 1979, and Esther died in 1981.

An early episode in Clyde Barrow's brush with Missouri's Route 66 occurred in the small town of Avilla. The Bank of Avilla was robbed on May 18, 1932, by members of the notorious "Irish O'Malley

Vintage postcard featuring the iconic ribbon of asphalt that was Route 66. *Courtesy of the author.*

Gang." The robbery also resulted in the kidnapping of the cashier, Mr. Ivy E. Russell, who was taken from the bank and driven toward Carthage, Missouri, where he was tossed out of the car and left by the roadside. Eventually, one gang member was sentenced to a seventy-five-year prison term for the Avilla bank robbery. Ivy E. Russell continued to manage the Bank of Avilla but increased security, keeping a firearm behind the teller window. A few months after the robbery, the Barrow Gang was in the area. The story is told that Clyde Barrow walked into the Bank of Avilla, looked Mr. Russell in the eye and spotted Russell's holstered pistol. He then supposedly tipped his hat, said "Afternoon" and promptly turned around and left. The Bank of Avilla was not robbed a second time.

Joplin's most-well known brush with Depression-era gangsters came in 1933, when Bonnie Parker and Clyde Barrow, along with other members of their gang, rented a garage apartment in south Joplin under assumed names. The Barrow gang had been in Joplin for about twelve days, and although they were already wanted in other states, they didn't seem too concerned about being recognized. Instead of lying low, the gang often went out to dinner. It is said that their favorite restaurant while in Joplin was Wilder's, which is still in business in the same location on Main Street.

In a sense, the real legend of Bonnie and Clyde was born in Joplin. The layover in Joplin is believed to have been set up by Clyde Barrow's brother Buck, who had been pardoned by the governor of Texas and released from prison one week before the gang showed up in Joplin. Joplin made a good

The post office in Avilla, Missouri, served as the Bank of Avilla during the Depression. Robbed by the O'Malley Gang, the Bank of Avilla took an offensive strategy toward bank robbery, which discouraged Clyde Barrow when he walked through the door. *Courtesy of the author.*

location for those on the run, as it was just a few miles from both the Kansas and Oklahoma state lines, and gangs could take advantage of the fact that law enforcement stopped at the state line in those days. The outlaws frequented Route 66 in southern Missouri, and Bonnie was very familiar with the area, having grown up in Commerce, Oklahoma, just a few miles across the state line.

To a nation weary of the harsh conditions of the Great Depression and a bit envious of the criminals, who were seen as fighting a system that was victimizing the people of the nation, Bonnie and Clyde were seen as folk heroes. What was left behind at their garage apartment, located at 3347 Oak Ridge Drive, only solidifies the legend. On April 13, 1933, suspicious neighbors, thinking that bootleggers had moved into the apartment, alerted the police. Five policemen responded with a search warrant just as Clyde Barrow and gang member W.D. Jones were arriving. In a shootout that lasted less than a minute, Barrow and Jones were injured and two officers shot. Newton County constable John Wesley Harriman and Joplin detective Harry McGinnis were mortally wounded. The other gang members, including Bonnie Parker, ran down

The Bonnie and Clyde garage apartment hideout in Joplin, Missouri, where two policemen were mortally wounded and film with the iconic images of Bonnie and Clyde was left behind. *Courtesy of the author.*

the apartment stairs, and the gang escaped in a stolen Ford V8 sedan. They left in such haste that Bonnie and Buck Barrow's wife, Blanche, left their purses. Stolen diamonds, which tied the Barrow gang to a robbery of a milling business in Neosho during their stay in Joplin, were also left behind. Bullet damage to the building still remains, particularly on the lintel over the garage door. One of Bonnie's poems was also left behind. The police also discovered undeveloped film containing candid pictures of Bonnie and Clyde—iconic images for which they are now remembered. The film was developed, and the pictures were printed in the *Joplin Globe* along with Bonnie's poem. The photos included a candid pose of Bonnie smoking a cigar and Clyde holding her up in the air. Another photo had Bonnie poking a sawed-off shotgun at Clyde's chest. These images gave Bonnie the reputation of a gun moll, although it is now accepted that she never shot a gun.

The Joplin apartment has for decades held a macabre interest, with many visitors wanting to drive by to get a glimpse of the building. I have heard of paranormal activity around the garage, and people often speak of a foreboding feeling. While it seemed the outlaws were living with a death

CITY of JOPLIN
POLICE PATROL DIVISION
JOPLIN, MISSOURI
WANTED

IDENTIFICATION
ORDER NO. 1201

BULLETIN ISSUED:
APRIL 25, 1933

FUGITIVES

CLYDE BARROW

FROM

BONNIE PARKER

JUSTICE

FUGITIVES

CLYDE BARROW

FROM

BONNIE PARKER

JUSTICE

Fugitive **MURDER** warrants have been issued for **Clyde Champion Barrow** & **Bonnie Parker**. In a shoot out with local authorities in Joplin, Mo., on April 13, 1933, Clyde Barrow is known to have killed Detective **Harry McGinnis** & Constable **J. W. Harryman**. Other members of the **Barrow gang** involved in the gun battle were Clyde's older brother **Marvin "Buck" Barrow** & W. D. "Deacon" Jones, a hometown friend & associate. Also present with the gang in a two story apartment house which they had sublet under assumed names was "Buck's" wife, **Blanche Barrow**. She is being sought as a material witness. All members of the **Barrow gang** are known to be **heavily armed** at all times & are **extremely dangerous.**
BULLETIN IN EFFECT UNTIL THESE PERSONS ARE CAPTURED OR DEAD. AUTHORITY--JOPLIN CHIEF OF POLICE

Reproduction of the wanted poster for Bonnie and Clyde issued by the Joplin, Missouri Police Department. *Courtesy of the author.*

wish (which can produce intense emotion), it is not clear that Bonnie and Clyde are responsible for the uneasy feeling experienced by visitors. It would seem more likely that the dying McGinnis and Harriman are responsible. Although the shootout at the apartment was tragic, the film found there

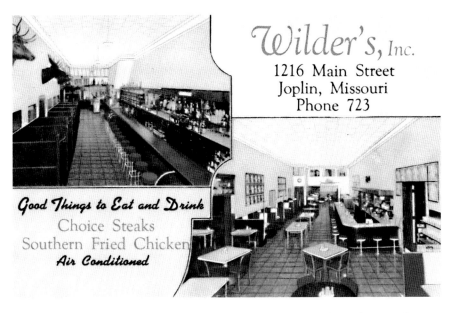

Wilder's Restaurant in Joplin, Missouri, has been a fixture on Main Street for more than eighty years and was reputed to be Bonnie and Clyde's favorite restaurant in Joplin. *Courtesy of the author.*

contributed to the creation of the legend that Bonnie and Clyde became in the ensuing decades. Those unforgettable images also contributed to their deaths, for it was with the same photos that law enforcement was able to track them down and ultimately kill them in a grisly ambush in Louisiana a year after Bonnie and Clyde left Joplin.

Bonnie and Clyde were well acquainted with Route 66. Following is a detailed account of Springfield motorcycle officer Thomas A. Persell's encounter with the Clyde Barrow gang as relayed to Perry Smith of the *Springfield Press* on January 27, 1933. The previous day, at about 6:00 p.m., Persell had stopped a Ford with Oklahoma license plates and, on approaching the driver's window, found himself at the wrong end of a sawed-off shotgun.

> *A few minutes before 6 o'clock Thursday night, as I was cruising near the corner of Kimbrough Avenue and St. Louis Street, I noticed suspicious actions of three persons in a V-8 model Ford coach. A girl was riding in the front seat with two men, and they looked as if they were trying to spot a car. They slowed down near a car with a Washington license which was parked in front of the Shrine Mosque but continued west on St. Louis Street. A short time later, I saw the machine turn east on Mitchell Street,*

in the rear of the Mosque. Becoming suspicious, I rode there and turned off my lights, and a few minutes later they returned and went north over the Benton Avenue viaduct. I pulled up beside the machine and ordered the driver to stop, but he declared that he didn't have any brakes. At the end of the viaduct, he turned east on Pine Street and stopped, and I noticed that the girl had got into the back seat of the car. Her arm was laying on the back of the seat and she had something in her hand. But I didn't know until later that it was a .45 army automatic. As I pulled up beside the machine, the driver stepped out with a sawed-off automatic shotgun in his hand and ordered me to hold up my hands and step into the car. He jerked my gun out of the holster and threw it to his companion in the front seat.

As I get in the front seat, the man with the gun swung around and shouted to a boy across the street "Get the hell out of here," and as he got into the machine, I thought I saw the boy run down an alley. The driver was the only person who talked for a time, and he was quite profane. He asked me if I didn't know better than to stop a car with an out-of-state license, and I told him that that was what I was getting paid for. He then told me I would have to show him the way out of town. I told him to turn off Pine Street on Washington Avenue. We drove to Center Street and from there to National Avenue. We left National Avenue at Division Street and went to Glenstone. They appeared unacquainted with the streets.

We turned on Highway 66, toward St. Louis, but the driver asked me if there wasn't a road to cut across and hit near Joplin, and I told him there was. He then ordered the girl to look at a map, meanwhile turning back to Glenstone. We drove about a mile farther, and they ordered me to get into the rear seat, where they covered me with a blanket. The girl held her pistol on me, and we drove up to a filling station and the gasoline tank was filled. After leaving the filling station, they told me to climb over into the front seat again, and I did, breaking one of their suitcases in doing so. I also saw a veritable arsenal, bigger than the one at the police station, on the floor of the car when I climbed over. There were two rifles, two automatic shotguns, a Thompson sub-machine gun and a number of pistols, including mine.

The girl I sat beside for such short time was red-haired and not the least bit beautiful. She weighed about 110 pounds, was freckled, as red-haired girls often are, and was wearing a dark coat and sort of a turban-like hat on the side of her head. Another suspicious thing about them was the great amount of money I saw in the back of the car. There were several sacks of coins, and I sat on two, which were under the blanket. There also was a bag in the front seat, which I thought contained some money. Just before we got to Crystal Cave, we turned onto the Pleasant Hope Road, and the driver batted along on that rough, winding road about 50 miles an hour. The driver seemed to be the leader, and he ordered the girl, whom he invariably addressed as Hon or Babe, to look at the road map and tell him which highways they were near. The other fellow, a silent sort of a chap, addressed the girl as Sis, and she called him Bud.

After leaving Pleasant Hope, we hit Highway No. 13, somewhere between Brighton and Bolivar. We rode on about two miles and turned on another rough country lane. I don't believe we drove more than 15 miles on the highway. The roads we traveled were muddy, but the driver hit about 50 miles an hour all along. We passed through the edge of Morrisville and near Greenfield met a car, which we apparently crowded into a ditch. The lights on our car weren't so good, and I think that was what caused the driver to nearly hit the other machine. Near Greenfield, they asked me how I happened to stop them and whether I had seen them fooling around the car, and I told them that I just stopped them to investigate their licenses. That was my only alibi. They then told me that they had stolen a car at Springfield Thursday afternoon, and, according to the description and license number they gave, it was the one taken from M. Kerr, a brown Ford V-8. But they said they ditched the machine out in the country and told me it was near a cemetery, probably out Campbell Avenue and Mount Vernon they said.

They put me back in the rear seat when we neared Golden City, and while we were parked at a garage there to get some gasoline, a night watchman came by and flashed his light over the car. The driver got out, and the man in the car said, "Look at that Hoosier." He laughed, and I peeped out from under the blanket and saw the watchman, but he went on without looking in the machine. It would probably have been too bad if he had tried to investigate. From Golden City, we went to another country road and came out on a highway. I saw a sign which said 7 miles to Jasper and 8 miles to Lamar. They knew all about the country around there and they dodged from one country road to another until we came to the residential district of Carthage. There, they indicated they were looking for a car to steal, and they drove around awhile and finally the driver asked the girl, "Hon, do you think there are any cars we can get at Webb City?" She answered in the affirmative, and they struck out across another country road and finally we came to the residential area of Webb City. The man who wasn't driving got out twice there but apparently was unable to get a machine, and finally we went to Oronogo. The driver said, "Hon, we know where there's a Buick here, don't we?" They seemed to know where they were going, but when they stopped, I saw a Chevrolet coach in front of a house. Neither of the men got out, and pretty soon they continued driving. While in Oronogo, the men kept talking about a gun battle and returning fire, and I asked, "Did they shoot at you?" One of the men said, "Yes—some monkey in the bank took a shot at us." We left town, and the next time I recognized my surroundings we were in a residential section of Joplin, the Roanoke district, I believe. There was a party going on at one house, and the man who wasn't driving got out and tried to get into five cars, which he classed as sorry because he couldn't start them. He opened a LaSalle sedan on one corner, but he couldn't find the switch. After that, he tried several more machines, but the girl claimed she saw a woman watching him out of a window and advised the driver to scram before police appeared.

We returned to Oronogo, and as we drove up the main street, one of the men said, "There's the bank, all lit up." The men seemed to have a mania for V-8 Fords, and I believe they were trying to steal the other cars just to get batteries for their machine. The driver returned to where the Chevrolet was parked, which had not been molested the first time, and he stopped his machine and got out but found it was locked. He disappeared a short time. When he came back, he said he had located a T-model Ford in a garage. Taking the Tommy gun and a pair of pliers, he went away again and was gone about 15 minutes. When he returned, he had an old battery, which was a sorry looking thing. He set it on the running board and started off. It fell off once, and we went back after it. After driving several miles, we stopped, and I held the light while the driver took the floorboards out of the car and prepared to put in the stolen battery. The other fellow stood behind me, and the girl stayed in the car. I helped with the pliers after he got the battery placed. I then took the light and walked around behind the machine with the second man, hoping to get a look at the license tags, but they were so mud-splashed I saw only the first three numerals. They were 406.

I had opened a package of cigarettes when I got into the car, and after smoking theirs, my companions began to mooch mine. The girl, who was as profane as her companions, simply ate fags. The driver didn't smoke. After throwing the old battery away, we turned the car around and drove about 6 or 7 miles, past some intersection. The driver then said, "Did you see that intersection?" and at an affirmative answer, he continued, "We're going to dump you here. You walk to that intersection, turn right and you'll come to a filling station and tourist camp. You can get a telephone there." They let me out at 12:30. I looked at my watch. But when I asked for my gun, the driver refused and said, "You're lucky as it is." I walked about 8 miles, but it seemed like a hundred before I got to the camp. There I called Joplin police and they sent a car after me. While I was talking with the tourist camp owner and his wife, they told me my former companions had held up the Bank of Oronogo recently. During our drive, I noticed they also avoided Ash Grove, Stockton and Lamar, and the driver once said about Ash Grove, "I had plenty of trouble there once." At Joplin, I called Desk Sergeant Henry Gardner and talked to Ruel Wommack, assistant chief of police here. Chief Wommack, Chief of Detectives Al Sampey and my wife drove to Joplin after me. I had arrived in Joplin about 2 o'clock.

The driver, who talked the most, seemed to be a foreigner of some sort. He was swarthy and appeared to be about 26 years old. He wore a tan hat and a dark suit. He weighed about 140 pounds. The other man was stocky built and seemed younger. He weighed about 160 pounds and was wearing a dark overcoat and suit. He also had on a dark hat. The little bit he talked about was the Tommy gun, of which he was quite proud. He said he had stolen it in Ohio. He also asked me about the speed of the police cars and whether the police and sheriff had machine guns in their arsenals. What I told them didn't help a bit.

In Springfield, there were two manhunts underway even though the assailants were not identified. The *Springfield News-Leader* reported:

[A] man leaving a grocery store witnessed Persell's kidnapping, and police were alerted. But Parker, Barrow and Jones got out of town before they could be spotted again. Hazel Persell was doing laundry at her parents' home when her father, C.W. Greenwade, was called and told Tom was missing. At first, her father wasn't going to tell her, but she sensed something was wrong and forced the information out of him. Her father, his dander up, recruited a neighbor, and both men took off in a car to try to find Tom. "I imagine he was well-armed," Tom W. [Persell] said of his grandfather. "He was quite an avid hunter." Hazel and Tom W. Persell said they are grateful her father did not cross paths with the well-armed outlaws holding her husband. Gunplay surely would have resulted.

Persell stated that Clyde Barrow brandished the sawed-off shotgun, as well as a roll of bills of money "big enough to choke a cow." Persell expected to be killed by his unknown kidnappers and could not pinpoint a reason as to why Bonnie and Clyde dropped him off on an isolated Jasper County

Facsimile of the April 15, 1933 edition of the *Joplin Globe* covering the shootout between police and the Barrow Gang that resulted in two officers dying. It was in the *Joplin Globe* that the famous images of Bonnie and Clyde were first published. *Courtesy of the author.*

road to walk away unharmed. His son later said, "Maybe it was because he kept cool even as he was forced to lie on the back-seat floorboard with Parker's heels digging into his back." He was released by the Barrow Gang at Poundstone Corner north of Joplin.

The newspaper continued:

As Persell stepped out of the gangsters' car, he brazenly asked them to return his gun, a Russian-made .45-caliber pistol he'd bought for $50 on his $105-a-month salary. "You've got all the guns you need," he told Clyde Barrow. But Barrow refused, saying, "We can use it." He also implied the officer was lucky to be alive.

The officer's revolver, which had unusual stag grips, was seen with Clyde Barrow in photos later developed from the film left at the Joplin hideout in April 1933. Ironically, it was from those photos that Persell was able to identify the Barrow gang as his captors. The experience of officer Persell demonstrates a familiarity with Missouri on and around Route 66 on the part of the Barrow gang. The Oronogo Bank incident mentioned by Persell had occurred less than two months earlier while the gang was hiding out in the Oronogo and Carthage areas for more than a month.

As time wore on, the Barrow Gang could no longer rely on anonymity, as their faces were now widely known from the film left in Joplin. That fame also meant that the outlaws had to be more ruthless and take more risks to outrun law enforcement. Missouri remained a favorite area of operation for Clyde Barrow, as Joe Gunn was to discover on February 12, 1934. Unlike Persell, Gunn quickly figured out who had forced him into a car at gunpoint, as described in the *Springfield Leader and Press* the following day:

Outlaws Take Two Men as Prisoners;
Kidnap Men on Wild Ride through Ozarks and Gun Battle with Officers;
WOMAN WITH BANDITS,
Bonnie Parker Laughs Gleefully as Bullets are Rained on Possemen.
February 13, 1934.

The notorious Barrow desperadoes kidnapped and later released two men. Their dash through the Ozarks country was interrupted yesterday by a gun battle with officers near Reeds Spring. The Texas outlaws, led by Clyde Barrow and his cigar-smoking sweetheart, Bonnie Parker, today were reported in the vicinity of the federal penitentiary at Leavenworth and the Kansas State prison, although southwest Missouri officers had expected them to head for the Oklahoma badlands after their trail was lost at Eureka Springs, Arkansas last night. Joe Gunn, 40, eccentric farmer who batches in the hills nine miles southwest of Reeds Spring, was a captive of the Barrows when they riddled an officer's car with machine gun and rifle bullets, he reported today.

Famished and fatigued when picked up on a highway near Reeds Spring at 11:30 o'clock this morning, Gunn described Barrow perfectly and identified Bonnie Parker by a small growth on her nose, which motorcycle officer Tom Persell had noticed when kidnapped by the Barrow gang a year ago. They rode in the front seat during the flight from officers, he said. In the back seat with Gunn, he said, were two men, one of whom officers believed was Raymond Hamilton, who escaped from a Texas convict road gang when Clyde and Bonnie battled the guard several weeks ago. A man, whose name Gunn did not learn, was kidnapped from the roadside at the edge of Berryville, Arkansas as the bandits fled south, and was released simultaneously with Gunn a few minutes later. Gunn said they both walked into Berryville without speaking. Gunn then described his solitary all-night walk back to Reeds Spring in a conversation relayed to Springfield by a telephone operator. Gunn's story this morning revealed that he was the man who sat in the car during the gun battle with officers, rather than Barrow, as officials had believed, and that Barrow himself had done most of the shooting. Gunn's report of his experience today revealed the inner story of the dash which began in Springfield when Mrs. George Thompson, 1304 East Walnut Street, saw two men roll the new Thompson sedan out of the driveway and speed away. She identified one of them as Barrow from his rogue's gallery picture. Not long afterward, the machine containing several persons roared through Hurley. Sheriff Tuttle was notified and picked up the chase at Galena, but the stolen machine was far in the lead when abandoned for Barrow's own maroon sedan before reaching Reeds Spring. J.O. Tolley, Reeds Spring school superintendent, saw them changing license plates and obeyed a signal to drive on. Sheriff Tuttle took charge of the stolen car, and Deputies Sam Thompson and Ernest Hayes continued the chase. City Marshall Dale Davis was waiting for the car at Reeds Spring. The Barrow gang, which already had picked up Gunn, saw the trap, stopped, shot until the deputies were out of ammunition, and then continued.

"I had been to a gristmill 2 ½ miles southwest of Reeds Spring and was walking back home on a side road when the bandits drove up beside me," Gunn recalled. "There was a man and woman in the front seat and two men in the back seat of the red car...one of the men got out of the back seat and asked me the direction to Berryville. Before I had time to answer, he had a gun on me and told me to jump in the back seat. I did, and we started out to the farm-to-market road between Reeds Spring and Cape Fair. We saw some officers coming and drove into another side road and found we were hemmed in." "We've got to let 'em have it, boys," Gunn quoted the small dark-complexioned man believed to be Raymond Hamilton, Texas fugitive, as he made selections from four automatic rifles. "There was a pile of shotguns in the back seat and enough ammunition to say mike," Gunn declared. Twice Clyde emptied his weapon, Bonnie reloading it while Gunn sat by, frightened stiff. As her sweetheart's machine gun threw a spray of perforations over the officer's car, the auburn-haired bandit queen was delighted, Gunn said.

Barrow gave the signal to drive away after the officers' ammunition was exhausted. Gunn said Hamilton climbed into the car, snickered and declared, "I sho tried to kill that _____ in back of the car!" Gunn believed he was referring to Deputy Ernest Hayes of Stone County, who was aided in the battle by Deputy Sam Thompson. Gunn said little conversation took place between the members of the gang during the 46-mile drive to Berryville. On the edge of Berryville, Hamilton left the car and approached a pedestrian, asking directions to Eureka Springs. The second victim, like the first, did not have a chance to answer before Hamilton started gunplay. Shanghaied into the front seat, the newcomer directed them toward Eureka Springs. About eight miles south of Berryville, Barrow stopped the machine, tweaked Bonnie's nose, and announced, "There's no use carryin' this dead weight, baby." The captives took their cue when nudged, Gunn said, and alighted.

Vintage photo of Clyde Barrow posing with a machine gun while sitting on the bumper of a stolen car. *Courtesy of the author.*

"We have been pretty good to you boys, so I want you to give us a 40-minute start," Clyde was quoted as demanding before his sedan rode away in a cloud of dust. It was about nightfall when the captives were liberated, and Gunn said the two walked back to the edge of Berryville without exchanging a single word.

Gunn, a community oddity, has never talked on the telephone, and his interview this afternoon had to be repeated by a telephone operator. He has other eccentricities, his friends at Reed Springs said. Gunn was found walking along the main highway 5 miles south of Reeds Spring shortly after 11 o'clock this morning by R.H. Sharp, a road contractor. His heavy cap, overcoat and overalls were ruined with dust, and he was famished and fatigued. Suede jackets, apparently belonging to Clyde and Bonnie, who are known to delight in them, were found in the recovered Thompson car. A man's hat was found at the site of the shooting.

Chapter 10

Billy Cook

Murder Hitchhikes on Route 66

The oldest cemetery in Joplin, Missouri, is the Peace Church Cemetery. Although it has suffered vandalism over the years, and broken tombstones are seen throughout, it isn't abandoned, and a surreal scene can be viewed when controlled burns are used to manage the thick prairie grasses that continuously threaten to reclaim the land. The first burial in Peace Church Cemetery predates the founding of the cemetery or even the church whose name it bears. When there were only a handful of settlers in the area, a trail passed nearby that was used by salt haulers to travel from the Springfield, Missouri area all the way to the western portion of Indian Territory (present-day Oklahoma) to the salt flats and return with salt. During one such trip, a slave of the salt hauler passed away from illness while the expedition was camped nearby. This spot was chosen for his burial because the men decided it had a nice view. Although the church has been gone many years, the cemetery has been in continuous use since the 1850s. It is a symbol of the early history of the area and continues to serve the needs of the community in honoring the dead.

Peace Church Cemetery has also become a destination for those seeking the thrill of risking a close encounter with the specter of evil and wickedness. Joplin native William Edward "Billy" Cook became the reason your mother warned you against picking up hitchhikers. He is buried at Peace Church Cemetery, but anyone unfamiliar with the events of his death will not find his unmarked grave.

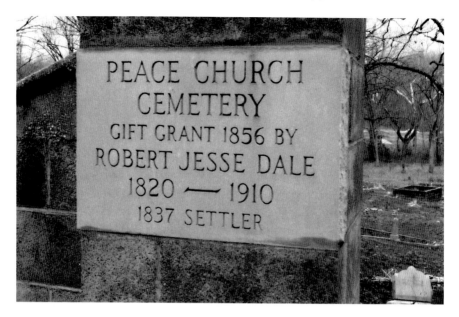

The main entrance of Peace Church Cemetery in Joplin, Missouri. The first burials here predate the cemetery itself. *Courtesy of the author.*

According to a December 22, 1952 *Time* magazine article:

> *When he was a five-year-old boy in Joplin, Missouri, William Edward "Billy" Cook was pushed out into the world on his own; his ne'er-do-well father abandoned him in a deserted mine cave. Because he had a deformed right eyelid, nobody wanted to adopt him. By the time Billy was 21, he had served time in both Missouri reform schools and the state penitentiary, had the words HARD LUCK tattooed on the fingers of his left hand and had resolved to "live by the gun." During a murderous 22-day rampage, Billy vented his rage at society.*

Billy Cook's life analyzed from a psychological perspective shortly after his death was that he did not have a close family experience—so common in the Midwest—due to his mother's death and father's abandonment as a consequence of "pathological alcoholism." The conclusion was that the deficiencies in his childhood led to psychopathic conditions, which in turn led to a life of delinquency. In their book *Psychopathy and Delinquency*, William and Joan McCord write, "In his few years of life, Cook had been a terrible scourge on society. His youth had been spent in fights, homosexual orgies, and robberies. His adult life, short as it was, had culminated in the killing of a fellow robber, in the murder of a husband and wife—and most shockingly—in the shootings of their two children."

In analyzing Cook's statements to psychiatrists after his capture, it seems very likely that Billy witnessed brutality and violence at home. His mother died under suspicious circumstances, and Billy recounted the discovery "with a typical insensitivity," according to William McCord: "One time my sister and me came home from playing at a yellow house and found her dead, lying on a cot. She had a large gash in the head." Researchers have concluded that it is probable that Billy's father murdered his mother. If Billy wasn't a psychopath initially, the violent death of his mother was the beginning of his transition into one. After their mother's death, the father then abandoned his children, leaving them to fend for themselves in a cave in Joplin, Missouri, until they were found and made wards of the juvenile court. The judge separated the siblings, the girls going to one home and Billy to another. Billy's foster mother sexually abused him. At the age of twelve, Billy ran away from his foster home but was captured by the police. The juvenile judge gave him the choice of returning to his foster mother or going to the state reformatory. Billy chose to be sent to the Missouri Training School. According to McCord, his summary of the experience was, "The training I received there was how to steal cars and pick locks." At seventeen, he was paroled from the Missouri Training School and lived briefly with each of his two now-married sisters, during which time his brothers-in-law helped him hone his criminal skills. One brother-in-law introduced Billy to brothels and further trained him in the skills of burglary, while the other found Billy a job only to steal his pay from him. Billy was charged with violating the terms of his parole and was found guilty based upon the testimony of one of his sisters. Billy was sent to the state penitentiary, where he became involved in fights, including one in which he attacked another inmate with a baseball bat, and became a "homosexual queen." Once again paroled, Billy returned to Joplin and attempted to reconcile with his father. He continued his criminal ways, and when the police came close to catching him, Billy told his father that he was going to "live by the gun." He left Joplin in 1950 and hitchhiked his way to California, ending up in the small desert town of Blythe, where he worked as a dishwasher in a diner—the only job he ever held for any length of time. There he met a woman named Cecilia who treated him with kindness.

In late December 1950, he drifted east to Texas and picked up a .32 caliber revolver. It was at this point that Cook began his twenty-two-day crime spree. On December 30, 1950, mechanic Lee Archer was driving near

Have You Heard the Latest One? They're Planning a Hotel at Camp Crowder, Apparently to House All the "Rumors" Afloat

Weather Forecast

JOPLIN NEWS HERALD Final Edition

Exclusive Day Dispatches of The Associated Press

SEVENTY-EIGHTH YEAR—NO. 266   JOPLIN, MISSOURI, MONDAY, JANUARY 15, 1951—TEN PAGES   PRICE 5 CENTS

FIND MOSSER BODIES HERE

BADMAN COOK IS CAPTURED IN MEXICO

Allied Troops Launch Sudden Offensive

Two Kidnaped Men Said to Be With Desperado

Joplin Ex-Convict, Suspected Slayer of Eight, Reported Seized 600 Miles Below Border

WILLIAM E. COOK, JR.

Hourly Temperatures
A cloudless sky brought warmer temperatures to Joplin and the district today, and the weatherman says it will remain fair

Gain Up to 12 Miles on the Western Front

Army Chief Collins Says U. S. Will "Stay and Fight"

Tokyo, Jan. 16—(AP)—American and Allied forces gained up to 12 miles Monday in a sudden offensive on the western Korean front south of Seoul.
Tank-infantry teams by

Recovered From Old Mine Shaft

Had Been Bludgeoned; Father and Son Shot;

downtown Joplin on Fourth street.
Police and FBI agents said there was no doubt but that the bodies were those of the Mossers and that all five had been brutally murdered.

The father, Carl Mosser, and his 7-year-old son, had been shot in the head. Gary Carl, 5 years old, and Pamela Sue, 3, apparently had been beaten to death. The wife and mother, Mrs. Thelma Mosser, had been bound, beaten, gagged and it was not immediately determined if she had been shot.

Dr. W. W. Hurst, coroner, said the bodies probably had been in the shaft at least 10 days.

Dim car tracks were found near the shaft, which had been boarded over. Police and FBI agents said it appeared that the bodies had been hauled to the shaft through a winding road off West Third street, and dumped in.

ALL BODIES ARE CLOTHED

Facsimile of the January 15, 1951 edition of the *Joplin News Herald* picturing William "Billy" Cook. *Courtesy of the author.*

Lubbock, Texas, when he picked up Billy Cook. Cook robbed Archer of $100 at gunpoint and forced him into the trunk of his car. Archer was able to escape by forcing open the trunk with a tire iron and jumping out as Cook made a slow turn onto a secondary road. After the car ran out of fuel on the highway between Claremore and Tulsa, Oklahoma, the extent of Cook's mental instability soon became apparent. After ditching Archer's car, he got a ride with the Mosser family, who were on vacation en route to New Mexico from Illinois. It was common to hitchhike and to pick up hitchhikers at that time, and Carl Mosser probably didn't think twice about helping out the young man. Cook forced Mosser to drive around aimlessly for three days. At one point, Mosser nearly wrestled the gun from Cook at a filling station near Wichita Falls, Texas, but Cook overpowered him. Finally, Mrs. Mosser and the children started crying hysterically. Cook responded by killing the Mossers, their three small children and even the family dog. Cook then drove the car to Joplin and dumped the bodies in an abandoned mine shaft outside the city. The car was later found in Oklahoma, blood-soaked and its seats torn from bullet holes. But Cook made a fatal mistake in leaving the receipt for the revolver he purchased in Texas in the Mosser car, and authorities now had a name for their suspect.

After the Mosser murders, Cook returned to Blythe, California. Deputy Sheriff Homer Waldrip became suspicious that the Billy Cook his wife, Cecilia, had worked with was the man described in the wanted bulletins sent out from law enforcement in Oklahoma. Waldrip went to the motel Billy had lived at when working at the diner to question the man with whom he had roomed. He was surprised to be met at the motel room door by Cook. Taken by surprise, Waldrip was taken hostage and held at gunpoint with his own gun. As with Carl Mosser, Waldrip was made to drive around in a random route. After driving about forty miles, Cook ordered the deputy to pull over. He made Waldrip lie face down in a ditch and told him that he was going to shoot him in the back of the head. While Waldrip awaited the gunshot, Cook walked back to the deputy's patrol car, got in and drove away. Later, when asked why he didn't shoot Waldrip, Cook told reporters that it was because the deputy's wife, Cecilia, had been nicer to him than anyone ever had.

After he left the sheriff, Cook then kidnapped another motorist, Robert Dewey, of Seattle. At some point while driving in the California desert, the traveling salesman tried to wrestle the gun from Cook but was wounded in the process as the car swerved off the road. Cook murdered Dewey with a shot to the head and left his body in a ditch. Cook then kidnapped James Burke and Forrest Damron, who were on a hunting trip. He forced the two men to drive across the Mexican border, where they eventually ended up in the small town of Santa Rosalia. By this point, law enforcement throughout the Southwest was looking for Cook. He couldn't outrun the bulletins circulating about him. Cook was recognized by Santa Rosalia police chief Luis Parra, who walked up to Cook and grabbed the .32 revolver from his belt before Cook could react. Cook was placed under arrest and returned to the border, where FBI agents were waiting to take him into custody. "I hate everybody's guts," Cook said at the time of his arrest, "and everybody hates mine." Cook admitted to the murders, stating that he didn't understand what the all the commotion was about and that he was just trying to avoid trouble.

Ironically, the same day that Cook was apprehended in Mexico, the bodies of the Mosser family were recovered in Joplin. Cook was returned to Oklahoma to stand trial for their murders. He underwent psychological testing, and seven psychiatrists gave their opinions to the court regarding Cook's competency to stand trial. He was found to be isolated from other people, lacking guilt (even in the killing of the Mosser children), extremely aggressive and preoccupied with his rejection by others. Three of the psychiatrists concluded that he was competent to stand trial, while four concluded that he was not. The

Image taken from a facsimile of the January 15, 1951 edition of the *Joplin News Herald* picturing the recovery of the bodies of the Mosser family, for whose murders Billy Cook was convicted and sentenced to three hundred years in prison. *Courtesy of the author.*

confirmed diagnosis was that Billy Cook was a psychopath. The judge made his own compromise, ruling that Cook was competent enough to stand trial but not competent to be put to death. Cook was convicted of murdering the five members of the Mosser family and sentenced to three hundred years in prison. In pronouncing the sentence, the judge concluded, "Billy Cook is a symbol of society's failure." There was a bloodthirsty atmosphere, and the judge's insightful conclusion was lost in the passions of the time. Cook was then extradited to California to stand trial for the murder of the Seattle salesman, Robert Dewey. He was convicted and sentenced to death. Cook was remanded to death row at San Quentin prison.

During his time at San Quentin, Cook crossed paths with Edward Bunker, who later became an actor and successful author and screenwriter. Bunker shared a similar childhood with Cook and was in and out of prison until 1975, when he was released and turned to writing. In his memoir, *Education of a Felon*, Bunker describes attacking Cook while in the showers with a shank, cutting him several times before being hauled away into solitary confinement by guards.

On December 12, 1952, Cook was executed in the gas chamber at San Quentin. But Billy Cook was to be used by one more person even in death. Glen Boydstun, a mortician in Comanche, Oklahoma, had been around long enough to remember the crowds paying to see bullet-ridden bodies of old West outlaws. And more recently, in 1934, the body of "Pretty Boy" Floyd had attracted more than forty thousand paying visitors in Sallisaw, Oklahoma. A similar fate greeted the bodies of Ma Barker and Fred Barker when they were killed in 1935. Boydstun decided to try his luck at the death display of Cook in Comanche, despite the fact that the town had absolutely nothing to do with Cook or his crimes.

Boydstun contacted Will Cook in Joplin and disingenuously intoned that he would be willing to foot the bill for a proper burial for his wayward son. Will Cook signed his permission for Boydstun to claim the body at San Quentin, and the mortician pointed his hearse toward California. Three days after the execution, Cook's corpse—outfitted in a suit and tie—was on public display in Comanche. Boydstun was dissatisfied with the initial day's box office proceeds, so he added loudspeakers and, like a sideshow barker, urged people to see "the last American desperado." Thousands came on the second day, including busloads of schoolchildren. In all, as many as twelve thousand people eyed the body before Cook's siblings had had enough. They hired a lawyer, wrestled their brother's corpse away from Boydstun and returned it to Joplin. Under the cover of darkness, as to avoid the press, his body was interred in the family plot in Peace Church Cemetery. As this news spread, so too did public outcry and opposition to the now infamous killer being buried in the cemetery. Billy Cook's grave was quietly moved just outside the original grounds of the cemetery but still near the family plot.

Cook has become the focus of local occult interest over the years. It is common to go to the cemetery and find piles of items—flowers, notes, candles, etc.—left in various spots where people believe that Cook's unmarked grave lies, as if he were a teen idol. It has been rumored that teenagers at times have congregated in attempts to contact the soul of Billy Cook. In 1987, three seventeen-year-old boys from nearby Carl Junction, Missouri, had been engaging in animal sacrifices and ended up committing a "thrill-killing" of a nineteen-year-old acquaintance of theirs by beating him to death with a baseball bat. During the murder trial, it was rumored that the boys were involved in satanic worship and were somehow influenced by the spirit of Billy Cook to commit murder. The boys were convicted of murder.

BARKER GANG SHOOT-OUT "MA", SON FREDDIE DEAD F.B.I. MANHUNT ENDS

"Ma" Barber   Freddie Barker

Reproduction of a press release about the deaths of Ma Barker and her son Freddie during the longest shootout in FBI history. *Courtesy of the author.*

Billy Cook was the inspiration of the film noir classic *The Hitch-Hiker*. The plot mirrors the experience of the two men kidnapped by Cook and driven to Mexico. In the movie, two men on a fishing trip pick up a hitchhiker named Emmett Myers, who turns out to be a psychopath who has committed multiple murders. *The Hitch-Hiker* went into production on June 24, 1952. Director Ida Lupino was a noted actress. *The Hitch-Hiker* was her first hard-paced, fast-moving picture after four films about social issues.

Lupino interviewed the two men that Billy Cook had held hostage and got releases from them, as well as William Cook, Billy's father, so that she could integrate parts of Cook's life into the script. To appease the censors, she reduced the number of deaths to three. *The Hitch-Hiker* premiered on March 20, 1953. It was marketed with the tagline, "When was the last time you invited death into your car?"

There is another legend that Billy Cook was the subject of inspiration for the Doors classic song "Riders on the Storm." According to band member Robby Krieger, the song was modeled after "(Ghost) Riders in the Sky" and even contains sound effects such as rain and thunder. A darker theory has been rumored that the song's lyrics describe the exploits of Billy Cook.

The area where Billy Cook is buried in an unmarked grave at Peace Church Cemetery in Joplin, Missouri. *Courtesy of the author.*

"Riders on the Storm" was the last song recorded by the Doors before Jim Morrison died in July 1971. The song's lyrics raise the question, but whether there's any truth to the theory will probably never be known. Supporters of the theory point to the following verse:

> *There's a killer on the road;*
> *His brain is squirming like a toad;*
> *Take a long holiday;*
> *Let your children play;*
> *If you give this man a ride, sweet memory will die;*
> *Killer on the road, yeah.*

In his book *L.A. Despair: A Landscape of Crimes and Bad Times*, author John Gilmore details first-hand accounts of those who had encounters with Billy Cook from Los Angeles to Blythe, shortly before the killing spree began. One man's account is as follows:

> *The only light leaking into the alley was the sheen from a JESUS SAVES sign blinking orange and red across the dirty asphalt. Seventy-six-year-old Gerald*

Stewart remembers that night. "So black," he says, "you could hardly see your hand at your face. Bums that couldn't get into the mission slept against the back of a building behind Main. You had to be careful where you pissed."

Stewart says he'd been in the alley dozens of times, but that night, God had to be looking the other way. "I got the hell scared right out of me by the kid coming at me in the dark, right on top of me and twisting his hands around that length of pipe like rolling a paper to beat a dog. First thought I had was he's got a gun, figurin' I was seein' a barrel. It was 1950, and I remember it like yesterday. A couple days after Thanksgiving, it was."

"Soon as I could see his face, I recognized him. I had a janitor job at the Midnight Mission, and the kid had slept in the flop a cot or two down from mine. He'd watched me stick some bills in the sock of one foot, and he kept watchin', even layin' there with that one eye open in the dark. Gave me the damn heebie-jeebies, that street lamp shining in and near lightin' that eye he didn't close." It wasn't a gun the kid had, only a hunk of pipe, "and squeezin' it like getting' ready to bust my head," says Stewart. "He had tattooed words on the fingers of his hand, and I didn't know which was worse to die by—bein' shot or gettin' my brains knocked in. He had a look the same as a dead man you got propped on its feet, and he was sayin', "I want you to know I ain't eat nothin' since day before yesterday. I've been on this sidewalk, and I hate this stinkin' city more'n I hate anything."

"What do you hate about it?" I asked. "You got free turkey and gravy two nights ago, didn't you?" I said, trying not to show he worried me. He kept lookin' me in the eye, and he said, "I just told you I hate this stinkin' city," sayin' all that like he's telling the time of day, and I said, "Well, fella, I do feel for you. I ain't found no city that ain't stinking to me neither." He didn't say nothin', in fact, I figured I could say anything and he wouldn't've heard any of it, just a starin' with that eye, holdin' still like a damned cat fixin' on a rat. But I didn't feel like any rat with what I'd been through in the war... enough to make you puke the whole thing. Italy and damned Germany, and I was thinkin' it's a helluva way to go, a squint-eyed kid who looked like a fire plug about to bust my head with a shit-house pipe."

Stewart dug in his pockets. "I tried savin' my hide and gave him what scratch I came up with. Maybe it was eleven bucks. Could've been less since I'd bought and drunk a pint before goin' in the alley to piss, and then him spottin' me where I'd gone, like he was a black shape comin' out of the shadows. I'd also bought smokes and just about was doin' my business when he was standin' there, same kid that'd wolfed the grub at the mission."

After staring at the older man for several moments, the kid said, "I seen you coming in here down that end, and I said here's a regular guy that'll help me out 'cause I gotta get to Barstow."

Stewart said, "What the hell's in Barstow?" "This turn-around collar guy," the kid said, "gave me a card of a guy he knows there. Told me I can get fixed up with work in Barstow."

"Work?" Stewart said. "In Barstow? That's the middle of the damned desert."

Stewart handed him the crumpled bills. "He looked at it in my hand and kept looking like he was still contemplatin' the use of that pipe on me even though I was giving him the scratch. I said I was glad I ran into him before I spent it 'cause I always tried helpin' a fella. He said that was white of me, and he let go of the pipe—gave a toss, and it clanked on the alley and rattled as he walked away. Didn't say nothin' else. 'Course later, when I learnt from the newspaper who he was and all that stuff about him bein' the most dangerous man in the country, I knew I'd walked off with my life instead of layin' with my brains in the alley. After givin' him the bucks, I didn't go to the flop for fear he hadn't taken off for Barstow or wherever the hell he was goin'. I got my gear and nosed over to the Salvation Army to hear some singing about the Lord. I figured I owed the Son of God my life and I'd say a prayer of thanks for Him lettin' me live by sendin' that miserable boy on his miserable way."

So does Billy Cook linger in Peace Church Cemetery? People experience fear, anxiety and a sinking feeling as they walk in the cemetery, particularly at night. Shadow people are seen as a routine matter, often leaning out from behind the scattered trees and tombstones, watching the living. I have observed shadow people in the cemetery. However, they are most commonly seen in an area on the opposite side of the cemetery from Cook's unmarked grave. "Graveyard lights" or "ghost lights" have also been observed, appearing as balls of light floating in the air amid tombstones. Few people feel comfortable standing in the cemetery after dark. However, Billy Cook may not be the only source of these feelings. What few people know is that there are a number of unmarked graves of Civil War soldiers killed in the area buried in Peace Church Cemetery on the opposite side from Billy Cook, in the area where shadow people are often seen. Perhaps the soldiers and Billy Cook are in an eternal standoff, locked in their own personal battles with demons of the past. Regardless, if you wish to seek out the reason you

Upon close inspection, the tombstones in Peace Church Cemetery are scarred from fires used to clear the prairie grass. Beyond this area are unmarked graves of Civil War soldiers killed nearby. *Courtesy of the author.*

should pass up the hitchhiker on the side of the road as you pass through Joplin, Missouri, on Route 66, stop at Peace Church Cemetery and see if the steely gaze of murderous rage stares back at you.

Chapter 11

Jesse and Frank James

Missouri's Sons and Outlaws

Perhaps Missouri's most famous sons were Jesse and Frank James. Route 66 follows the James brothers' trail across Missouri.

The Pinkerton detectives killed the Jameses' eight-year-old half brother and maimed their mother, her arm having to be amputated, in the fervor to kill the James brothers by throwing a bomb through the front window of the family farm in Kearney, Missouri. Bob Ford, a member of the James Gang, shot Jesse James in the back in Jesse's own house while James stood on a chair straightening a picture frame, only to never be paid the promised reward. However, neither the Pinkertons nor the Ford brothers were the first to pursue the James brothers for the substantial reward on their heads.

The Carthage Patriot reported on the speculated murder of Jesse James near Joplin, Missouri, on November 6, 1879. Following is the article in its entirety:

JESSE JAMES, Reported Killing of This Noted Outlaw

The following accounts we take from the Joplin Herald. Late Sunday evening [November 2, 1879], a report reached Joplin that Jesse James, the noted out-law, had been killed near Short Creek by George Shepherd, a member of the gang. [Jasper County] Sheriff McBride and some other parties immediately started for Short Creek, and upon their arrival there found the town in a great state of excitement. Shepherd was found at a hotel with a bullet wound in his leg, and his statement was that he had killed Jesse James outright and had been wounded in

Jesse James as he looked during the height of his bank-robbing days. *Courtesy of the author.*

escaping from the rest of the gang, which was composed of Jesse James, Jim Cummings, Henry Miller and another man he did not know, and that they had planned a robbery at Empire [Kansas]. The scheme was for Shepherd to ride to Empire, find out how the land lay, and return. He states that his intention was to give the whole thing away and have the party captured when they came into town, but he afterwards changed his mind and told the Clary brothers and Jim Flanery about the matter. The four men then arranged a plan to lead the robbers into an ambush and kill or capture them. Three of the men were to hide in a ravine, and Shepherd was to lead the gang that way and assist in shooting them when the other party opened fire.

About eight o'clock, Shepherd left Short Creek, and after traveling about six miles in a southern direction, he found the trail of the party, who had left their camp. Between 9 and 10 o'clock, he caught up with them near Lee's farm, nearly a mile from the crossing on Shoal Creek. When Shepherd rode up to Jesse James, the latter said, "It is rather suspicious about you staying so long." Shepherd quickly placed his pistol at the back of Jesse's head, and with the remark "This is for killing Ike Flannegan," shot him dead. He then started on a mad gallop in a southern direction, hoping to lead the rest of the party near the ambush. One of the party rode to the dead man, and the others immediately started in pursuit of Shepherd. Owing to the swiftness of his horse, he distanced one of them, but Cummings, who rode a powerful horse, gained on him rapidly, firing all the time with his revolver, hitting him once in the calf of the leg. Seeing that he was going to be overtaken, Shepherd wheeled his horse and rode toward Cummings. Both men fired rapidly as they approached each other, and Shepherd says he is quite sure he shot Cummings in the breast. When they got close to each other, Shepherd's horse sprang against a tree, and in trying to get control of him, he dropped his pistol to the ground. Cummings' horse dashed through the woods with him, and before he could get him turned around, Shepherd was speeding away out of reach of his pistol. Shepherd then rode into town and gave the alarm. An effort was made to organize a party to search for the dead man, but it was nearly dark before they could reach the spot where the shooting was done. A telegram was sent to Marshall Liggett, of Kansas City, and he at once started down in a special train with a company of trusty men. The train arrived yesterday morning at two o'clock, and at daylight, a posse of men accompanied by Deputy Sheriff Ross started on the trail of the robbers.

Shepherd knew the James brothers in Kentucky, nearly ten years ago, and he assisted them to escape after they had committed a bold robbery at Russellville, in that state. For this offense, he was convicted and sent to the penitentiary for three years. In after years, he moved to Kansas City, and has been connected to the James brothers ever since. Not many years ago, Jesse James killed Flannegan, a nephew of Shepherd's, and he claimed the revenge which, according to his statement, he has wiped out in blood.

There is a great difference in opinion in regard to Shepherd's story, and if a man in Joplin wanted to bet any money that Jesse James was dead, he could get accommodated right away. Many citizens think that the gang *suspected Shepherd of treachery, and when he returned, attempted to kill him. There has been nothing found that will point to the death of Jesse James. The public generally will not believe that he was killed, but there is one thing about it—Shepherd has undoubtedly been with the James gang and had some kind of collision with them, but whether he shot anyone remains to be proven.*

Yesterday evening, a Herald reporter met Dr. Burns in East Joplin and in conversation with him learned that he was at Mr. Lee's residence last Sunday, near Shoal Creek, when the shooting took place between Shepherd and the robbers. He said he saw a man riding down the road towards the ford at a full gallop and that he held the bridle rein in his teeth and a revolver in each hand. In a few moments, some excited neighbors came up the road and said they had met a man riding toward Shoal Creek with a revolver in each hand and that he had halted them in the road and told them that he had shot a man in the woods. Directly, some other neighbors came from the opposite direction and said that a man had been killed not far from there, and some men were carrying off the body. The doctor stated he was within fifty feet of Shepherd when he rode along and that he was wounded in the leg. He also described Shepherd as having but one eye and said that the horse he rode was either a very dark bay or black. This in part substantiates Shepherd's story, but in other particulars, there is a confliction. Shepherd says he lost his pistol in the woods, and Dr. Burns says he had one in each hand as he gallop[ed] toward Short Creek. There is a mystery surrounding this affair which time alone will clear up, and by tomorrow, the Herald hopes to give its readers a full history of the tragedy.

There is a $15,000 reward for the James boys.

Deputy Sheriff Ross is with Marshal Liggett and his posse in search of the James gang. Nothing has been heard from them direct since yesterday, and it is supposed they have gone down into the Nation [Indian Territory, in present-day Oklahoma].

IS JESSE JAMES DEAD?
That is the All-Absorbing Question of the Day
The Patriot Believes that He Was Shot if not Killed
The Latest News From Joplin Concerning the Affair

There are so many rumors afloat concerning the highly sensational report of the killing of Jesse James near Short Creek on Sunday last that the truth is hard to be obtained. The people in general seem to put but little confidence in the report throughout, but all the officers and those in a position to know are positive that the story as first given out and as published in yesterday's Patriot is true. The daily papers of Joplin are both quite positive that James was shot and most probably killed. A Patriot reporter interviewed Deputy Sheriff B.F. Thomas this afternoon, and he most emphatically said that it was his firm belief that Jesse James was killed by Shepherd last Sunday, and he proceeded at length to give his reasons for so believing. Sheriff McBride and his two deputies, Thomas and Ross, knew of the whole scheme that was being laid for the capture of the gang by officer Liggett, of Kansas City, through the aid of the man Shepherd. They also knew that at or about Short Creek was to be the scene of the encounter. They knew that Liggett had a special train of cars standing on a side track at Kansas City for two or three days awaiting a telegram from Shepherd. Sheriff McBride and Deputy Ross had been making their headquarters in Joplin for several days, awaiting a telegram from Liggett to move at a moment's notice with a body of picked men to the scene of action. Sheriff Bahney of Columbus, Kas., was also holding himself in readiness for quick movements. Arrangements had been made for a guard at every road and footpath for miles surrounding the Short Creek country. Everything was in readiness for a certain sweep of the James gang the moment that Shepherd would give the signal to Liggett. When Shepherd left Liggett nearly two weeks ago, his last words were, "I will get the whole gang so that we can capture or kill them, if possible, and if I fail in that, I will kill Jesse James anyway." As the sequel shows, the plan did not work, and Shepherd tells the reason: When about two days' ride from Short Creek where they were going to rob the office of W.J.L. & Z. Co., Shepherd entrusted the telegram to Liggett to a friend living on the route—that friend failed to send it as agreed upon. Upon arriving at Short Creek, the gang found out that there was not money enough to justify them robbing the W.J.L. & Z. office, and they moved on southwest. Shepherd also found that a screw was loose somewhere, or Liggett and his party would be somewhere in the vicinity, and of course he at once concluded that Liggett had not got the dispatch. Shepherd, seeing his game was up at this point, determined to carry out his threat to kill James at all hazards. Liggett is now in Short Creek and confirms every word Shepherd has said, so far as he knows. Every statement made by Shepherd corroborates with what information the sheriffs of this county have been cognizant of, and not a single flaw or misstatement has yet been discovered. Deputy Thomas tells the Patriot *reporter that a dispatch went over the wires to St. Louis last night, stating that the place of the fight had been found and that the trail where a dead body had been dragged from the road was clearly seen.*

Last evening's Joplin News says:

"Marshal Liggett, of Kansas City…is confident that the story related by Shepherd is strictly true. He says Shepherd's word may be relied upon—that he is a man of as much nerve as the James boys were ever credited with, and so far as he (Liggett) has investigated the matter, he is confident that Jesse James was either killed outright or very dangerously wounded and that he had a posse started out from Short Creek immediately upon Shepherd's arrival there on Sunday. James' body might have been recovered, and probably the capture of his companions effected. As it was, the party had ample time to bury or conceal the body, if James was killed, and to get out of the way of any pursuing party that might venture into the brush after them, and the recovery of the body is now a very doubtful question, though Liggett's men are still on hunt of it and in pursuit of the gang."

Shepherd's wound, though painful, is not very serious, and he was to have left Short Creek today for Kansas City, where he resides. When our reporter saw him yesterday at the Banks Hotel, he was lying in bed, his head propped up by a chair. On either side of him, under the cover, lay a navy revolver. Upon it being suggested that someone ought to guard his room, as some of James' friends might give him an unwelcome visit, he remarked, "Well, they won't get away with me very much,' saying this he showed how he was "fixed" for them.

We take the following interviews and comments from this morning's Joplin Herald:

Why a man possessed of his natural senses should rush into town and spread the false report that he had shot and killed one of the most notorious outlaws in America, no man in this part of the country can figure out, and yet at this present writing, the general opinion prevails that George Shepherd's story was simply a canard. As far as the Herald *has been able to learn, Marshall Liggett, and a very few other men, are the only parties who believe that Jesse James was killed. The whole affair is shrouded in an impenetrable mystery, and it is very doubtful if the public will ever know just the true facts in the case. That Shepherd had an encounter with the robbers and got wounded himself, few very people doubt, but the public mind in this vicinity is incredulous on anything more.*

Yesterday, a Herald *reporter interviewed several parties in regard to the affair, and not a single man could be found who believed that Jesse James had been killed.*

DEPUTY SHERIFF PAYTON

was the first man approached, and the reporter opened the conversation by asking Mr. Payton what he thought of the shooting.

"Well, I'll tell you," said the gentleman, "I saw Shepherd, and he said he was positive he had killed Jesse James, but for all that I do not believe that he did. Shepherd's story was straight enough, and he looked like a man telling the truth, but still I can not swallow his statements."

"How do you think Shepherd got shot?"

"Oh, I think the gang suspected him, and perhaps had been informed of his treachery, and when he returned, they opened fire on him, and by a mere miracle he escaped. He undoubtedly had a running fight with them, but I think he was the only man shot."

"Were you near where the shooting was done, Mr. Payton?"

"Yes, I was within about a mile of the place, but I could discover no trace of a man being killed."

"You saw Dr. Burns' statement in this morning's Herald?"

"Yes, I saw it, and it coincides exactly with what Shepherd says, for he brought two pistols into town. He said he had three in the first place, and lost one in the fight. Dr. Burns has a patient in that neighborhood, and his description of Shepherd is correct."

DR. BURNS,

The reporter met this gentleman in the post office late yesterday, and he simply reiterated his statements made in yesterday's paper. He said that the people in the neighborhood of Lee's farm had heard several shots fired and had also seen a party of men making off with the body of a dead man. The Dr. is firmly convinced that a man was killed, and that he saw the man who killed him.

FLETCH TAYLOR.

The above gentleman was encountered at the Joplin Hotel saloon, and the following interview took place:

"Mr. Taylor, do you believe that Shepherd killed Jesse James?"

"No, sir, I do not. I think Jesse James is alive and well this minute."

"What reasons have you for believing Shepherd did not tell the truth?"

"Well, in the first place, Shepherd's story is improbable from the fact that Cummings is a powerful man and a crack pistol shot. He could have shot Shepherd out of his saddle of a distance of twenty or thirty yards, and Shepherd says he missed him even when the fire from his pistol burned the overcoat on the saddle in front of him. It is an improbable story, and any one who knows anything about the James boys or anything of their gang would never be so rash as to attempt to escape their bullets after shooting one of their number."

Several other gentlemen were also interviewed, and they expressed themselves in a manner that showed they were in doubt about the death of Jesse James.

Many soldiers and guerrilla fighters used the skills they learned in the Civil War in later years either while breaking the law or enforcing it. Reenactment photo. *Courtesy of the author.*

George Washington Shepherd was born in Jackson County, Missouri, in 1842 and served in the U.S. Army during the Mormon War at the age of fifteen. He returned to farming in the vicinity of Kansas City, Missouri, two years later, but by the time he was seventeen years old, the Civil War broke out, and he joined the Confederate cause. He served in the Missouri State Guard and fought for the Confederate army under General Sterling Price in August 1861 at the Battle of Wilson's Creek, near Springfield, and the Battle of Pea Ridge, Arkansas, in February 1862. When the Missouri State Guard was absorbed into the Confederate army and retreated south into

Cole Younger (left) and Jim Younger, circa Civil War years. The Younger brothers were childhood friends of Myra Belle Shirley (later Belle Starr) and rode with the James brothers under William Quantrill and "Bloody Bill" Anderson. *Courtesy of the author.*

Arkansas, Shepherd elected to stay in Missouri and fight as a guerrilla fighter under William Clarke Quantrill. It was as a member of Quantrill's Raiders that Shepherd became acquainted with the principals of the future outlaw James Gang. Frank and Jesse James, as well as Cole, John and Jim

REWARD
☞ $10,000.00 ☜
Wanted DEAD or ALIVE!
The Notorious Outlaws
FRANK AND JESSE JAMES

These men are wanted in connection with the robberies of several banks and trains, and the cold-blooded murder of several innocent citizens. These are bold and dangerous men, and caution should be taken when approaching them.

IMMEDIATELY CONTACT
NEAREST U.S. MARSHAL'S OFFICE

Reproduction of the wanted poster for Frank and Jesse James issued by the U.S. Marshals Office. The large reward offered for the James brothers marked them for murder even before Bob Ford shot Jesse James in St. Joseph, Missouri. *Courtesy of the author.*

Younger, fought under Quantrill and were well acquainted with Shepherd, one of Quantrill's lieutenants. Several of Shepherd's relatives served under Quantrill, including his nephew, Isaac "Ike" Flannery. It appears that it is Ike Flannery that the foregoing newspaper article was actually referencing,

Vintage photograph of Jesse James taken during the Civil War, at which time he was a bushwhacker riding under William Quantrill and "Bloody Bill" Anderson and operated in southern Missouri on roads that later became part of Route 66. *Courtesy of the author.*

not Flannegan. After Quantrill was killed during the Civil War, many of his men followed "Bloody Bill" Anderson, including most of the principals mentioned above.

It appears that Shepherd and others genuinely believed that he had killed Jesse James, as reported later in the *Joplin Herald*:

Mrs. Samuel's Say
Joplin Daily Herald, *July 22, 1880*
Racy Interview Between the Mother of the James Boys and Geo. Shepherd

Mrs. Samuels, mother of the notorious outlaws, Frank and Jesse James, resides in a small house situated among the timber near Kearney, a small station on the Hannibal and St. Joseph Railroad, a few miles from Kansas City, and can always be expected in this city within twenty-four hours after any startling news appears regarding her outlawed sons. On Saturday last, the Times contained an article regarding the appearance of Frank James in the eastern portion of the county, and yesterday, like the "Lone Fisherman," Mrs. Samuels appeared at the office of County Marshal Liggett, the look of inquiry in her face plainly telling what she came for. After talking with the Marshal awhile, Mrs. Samuels managed to ask some questions regarding the reported appearance of Frank and then went to do some shopping. She was on her way back to the Court House when a man from Liberty, knowing who she was, stopped her at the corner of Main and Fifth Streets and asked her "if she would like to see George Shepherd, the reported slayer of her son near Joplin last fall."

"Is he about here?" asked Mrs. Samuels, her whole frame showing the excitement which, like Banquo's ghost, would not down as the name of Shepherd was uttered.

"Yes, he is right here on the corner," and Mrs. Samuels was escorted where Shepherd was standing, near the barber shop just north of Fifth Street on Main.

Mrs. Samuels cast one contemptuous look at the man and then said: "As so George Shepherd, you say you killed my son Jesse?"

"Yes I did."

"What did you do it for?"

"Partly to avenge an old score and partly for money," replied the one-eyed ex-guerilla.

Mrs. Samuels all this time was eyeing the man before her, who boasts of having killed her son, and then asked quickly, "And so you killed Jesse, and do you expect to live until the leaves fall?"

"I think it doubtful."

"Well, I should think you would. George Shepherd, I would see my far [illegible] *and live the rest of my days in the poor house in order to raise money to pay someone for killing you if I knew you killed Jesse."*

As she said this, Mrs. Samuels became terribly excited, and Shepherd drew back in the hallway to continue the conversation, as a crowd had gathered, knowing that the mother of the most famous outlaws in the country was in conversation with the man who said to have followed and killed one of them at the risk of his own life. The two then continued the conversation, and those who witnessed it say that the old lady laid down the law in the most emphatic manner. At the conclusion of the confab, Mrs. Samuels moved away, repeating her vow that Shepherd would die before winter, "as money could accomplish anything."

Vintage postcard of Meramec Cavern. Located on Route 66 in eastern Missouri, the cavern served as a hideout for the James Gang at various times. *Courtesy of the author.*

Belle Starr, the "Bandit Queen," grew up in Carthage, Missouri, and knew the Younger and James brothers during the Civil War. Myra Belle Shirley was the daughter of John Shirley, a successful businessman and farmer, and attended the Women's Academy in Carthage, learning multiple languages and subjects of art and grace. She seems to be an unlikely bandit; however, the Battle of Carthage, on July 5, 1861, started a chain of events that led this young woman to the path of an outlaw.

The battle turned to urban guerrilla tactics, as it became a house-to-house fight. Among those civilians witnessing the fighting was fourteen-year-old Myra, who helped nurse wounded in the streets. The Shirley family, Southern sympathizers and slaveholders, had multiple tracts of land in Jasper County. Myra's father, John Shirley, owned the Shirley Hotel and tavern on the north side of the square. None of those pre-war buildings survived the war due to the town being burned multiple times. A plaque in the sidewalk commemorates the spot where the hotel was located. This was Myra's first brush with the violence of war, but not her last. Her older brother Bud joined the Confederate cause, fighting with bushwhackers, only to be shot while eating supper at a house in nearby Sarcoxie about a year after the Battle of Carthage.

Reproduction of a drawing depicting Belle Starr's escape from jail, which occurred much to the dismay of Isaac Parker, the "Hanging Judge." Belle honed her escape skills as a teenage Confederate spy during the Civil War in southern Missouri. On one occasion, she made a daring escape from Union soldiers through a second-story window at the Ritchey Mansion in Newtonia, Missouri. *Courtesy of the author.*

The Civil War caused horrific hardships on civilians and soldiers alike. Reenactment photo. *Courtesy of the author.*

The family retrieved his body and buried him secretly. Some say that he was buried at the old City Cemetery, where Central Park is now located. Most of the graves were moved to make way for the park, and those of soldiers killed in the Civil War were reinterred at the National Cemetery in Springfield, Missouri. However, it is known that not all of the graves were moved, as later, when digging to make way for improvements, more graves were unearthed. There are other stories of Bud being buried in various locations under the cover of darkness out of fear that enemies would desecrate the body. The Shirley family gave up their home and business and headed to Texas during the war, as did many other Southern sympathizers in southwest Missouri. Some speculate that Bud's body was dug up and taken to Texas with the family to be reinterred.

In 1866, Belle married James C. "Jim" Reed, a former guerrilla whom she had known since her childhood in Carthage. The couple's daughter, Rosie Lee "Pearl," was born in 1868, and their son James Edwin was born in 1871. Belle spent much of her time in saloons, drinking and gambling at dice, cards and roulette. At times, she would ride her horse through the streets, shooting off her pistols. In 1874, Jim Reed was shot to death while trying to escape from the custody of a deputy sheriff. Belle

Guerrilla fighters and bushwhackers during the Civil War were a familiar site in Missouri, and the violence carried over into the Reconstruction years. Reenactment photo. *Courtesy of the author.*

married Sam Starr and involved herself in planning and fencing for the rustlers, horse thieves and bootleggers, as well as harboring them from the law.

Judge Isaac C. Parker, aka the "Hanging Judge," of Fort Smith became obsessed with Belle Starr, but she eluded him at every turn. Then, in 1882, Belle and Sam were convicted of horse theft, and Judge Parker sentenced Belle and Sam to a year in the House of Correction in Detroit, Michigan. During her prison term, Belle proved to be a model prisoner.

On February 3, 1889, two days short of her forty-first birthday, while riding near her ranch at Eufaula, Oklahoma, Belle was killed by a shotgun blast to the back. Suspects included Edgar Watson, with whom Belle had been feuding over the land he was renting from her; her lover, Jim July, with whom she had recently had an argument; and her son Ed, with whom she had had a strained relationship. However, the murderer of Belle Starr was never identified.

Chapter 12

The "Stefflebeck" Bordello

The Staffleback House of Ill Fame and Gruesome Horrors

Technically, we have now wandered across the state line into the extreme southeast corner of Kansas, but only about a mile. There are only approximately thirteen miles of Route 66 in Kansas as it bends south toward Oklahoma. The story of the "Stefflebeck" Bordello is one that begins in Missouri and has its gruesome climax a stone's throw into Kansas. As you head west out of Joplin, Route 66 takes you off the highway via the road marked simply "Old Route 66." As you slow to accommodate the aging road surface, you immediately step back in time, and it's easy to conjure the iconic ribbon of concrete as it originally looked along this stretch of meandering two-lane pavement. Open and closed small businesses line the drive, many with Route 66 displayed in their names. As you approach the state line, mid-century life gives way to an open expanse of mining land, sitting just as it has for almost a century. In the midst of this open expanse rises a concrete bridge, resembling the rolling hump of a massive sea serpent breaching the expanse of "chat"—gravel left from the tailing piles of long-defunct lead and zinc mines that dot the area. On closer inspection, you can see below the bridge where a rail line once kept the mining field bustling and forced Route 66 to travel the miniature roller coaster rise overhead. Next, you come to a stop sign at Main Street in Galena, Kansas. On this corner, to your right, stands the "Stefflebeck" Bordello at 203 North Main Street. Ironically, juxtaposed across the street to the south is the Four Women on the Route store, at which sits the old International truck that was the inspiration for the character Tow Mater in the Pixar animated movie *Cars*. Here at this

The sign on Old Route 66 at the Missouri/Kansas state line. *Courtesy of the author.*

The Stefflebeck Bordello as it now sits. In the background lay the mineshafts in which evidence of the murder victims was found. *Courtesy of Paranormal Science Lab.*

unassuming intersection on Route 66, images of childhood innocence and cold-blooded murder face off in silence.

Today, as you drive through Galena, Kansas, it is hard to imagine this small town of three thousand having at least ten times that number of residents, but that was the case in the 1890s. During this time, thirty thousand people, many single, transient men, were busily seeking their fortunes in the booming lead and zinc mining fields in and around Galena, which flowed west contiguously from the mining fields of Joplin, Missouri. But don't make the mistake of assuming things were simpler in those days. Many entrepreneurs figured out in the Joplin mining district, as well as other mining towns across the western United States, that there was more money to be made from providing goods and services to the miners than trying their own hand at mining. One such enterprising businesswoman set up a thriving bordello on this corner of Main and Fort Streets in Galena. Although generally known as Ma Stefflebeck, her name was actually Nancy Staffleback. How the misnomer of Steffelbeck arose is uncertain. What is apparent, however, is that Nancy did not start out as a madam or criminal of any sort.

Nancy was born in New York in 1833, and her maiden name was Chase. She married Swiss immigrant Michael Staffleback, fifteen years her senior, in Iowa, and the couple subsequently settled in Lawrence County, Missouri, where years later, Route 66 would bisect the county. At some point, the family moved to Joplin and settled in the Swindle Hill section of town. The name was not a slur for a rough area of town; it was named for Jacob Swindle, who owned a large tract of land there and prospered in the 1870s in the early Joplin mining fields. In the 1880 Census, Michael Staffleback was listed as a candy maker residing in Joplin, Missouri, and Nancy was listed as a midwife. At that time, six of the couple's thirteen children still resided with them, including twelve-year-old Michael, who appears to be Mike Staffleback, later to participate in the infamous murders.

It is unknown what propelled the Stafflebacks into a pattern of crime. The earliest account of a run-in with the law dates to July 1878, but not for criminal activity per se. Michael and Nancy's twenty-one-year-old son Johnny apparently had mental instabilities that included some sort of delusions or hallucinations. According to Larry Wood,

Johnny Stafflebac[k]...went on the warpath in the Joplin neighborhood where the family lived at the time, breaking furniture and threatening to kill "an imaginary enemy." The young man's father, Michael Stafflebac[k], fearful that his "insane son" would hurt himself or others, had to enlist the help of neighbors to subdue the twenty-one-year-old Johnny. Johnny often created disturbances on the streets in the past during similar "crazy spells."

Johnny's fate is unknown, for two years later he is not included in the household with his parents and siblings in the 1880 Census. However, the fact that mental illness was present in the family may partially explain later events.

Ed Staffleback, who would become a cold-blooded murderer in the 1890s, married his wife, Mattie, in the early 1880s. Mattie is not in the picture by the time Ed and the other Stafflebacks start their murdering spree.

Mike Staffleback had multiple run-ins with the law in Lawrence County, Missouri. *The Chieftain*, in Mount Vernon, Missouri, reported on June 21, 1894, "Mike Staffleback was brought up from Pierce City yesterday…and placed in jail, to walls of which he is no stranger. He is charged with the crime of burglary, which he is alleged to have committed near Clarkson about three months ago. He was caught at Joplin a few days ago and at the time of his arrest is said to have had on a suit of clothes he got while making the raid." Apparently, Mike was motivated to avoid a court hearing on the burglary charges, as reported by *The Chieftain* on August 2, 1894:

As circuit court cometh apace the prisoners confined in jail, whose cases will come before it, begin to grow restless. This nervous and anxious feeling possessed three prisoners last week: Bony Cox, Mike Staffleback and Harry Mitchell, colored. They made an almost successful attempt to escape and but for the watchful eye of Sheriff Wilson and his deputies, would have succeeded. In times past, a hole had been picked through the floor of the north cell, and to avoid escape by that route, the sheriff has been keeping it fastened at all times, but by some means, the prisoners had broken the bolts and got in and made the hole in the rock large enough to admit their bodies, and on the night of July 23, the above named got under the floor of the jail and were at the trap door under the stairway leading to the county clerk's office when caught and returned to their former home in the bastile. The hole in the floor has been covered with boiler iron and riveted with heavy bolts until it is no doubt safer than before the first hole was picked through.

It would appear that Mike was then convicted of those charges, as the following was reported by *The Chieftain* on September 13, 1894:

This paper stated that "Michael" Staffleback was sentenced to the penitentiary at the recent term of the circuit court. The father wishes a correction made, and we willingly comply. His name is plain Mike, and nothing more. The old gentleman is named Michael and as is natural does not wish any false impression sent abroad.

It can be speculated that the father's wish to distance himself from unlawful behavior was at least a factor leading to further estrangement. In 1895, Michael left the family, and he and Nancy subsequently divorced. It appears that it was at this point that Nancy started down the path of crime. In late 1895, Nancy became romantically involved with an old married man named Rosenbaugh. Many accounts during the later trial referred to the murder of an old man for his pension money. In *Ozarks Gunfights and Other Notorious Incidents*, Larry Wood writes, "On Christmas Day of 1895, Rosenbaugh started for the old woman's [Nancy's] shack at 1101 Ivy Street (now Connor) in Joplin with a large sum of money on his person and was never heard from again." Shortly after Rosenbaugh disappeared, the Stafflebacks moved on to Galena.

The "Old Tavern," built in 1868 in Avilla, Missouri, is a good representation of the saloons and gambling parlors popular in the late 1800s along the future Route 66. *Courtesy of the author.*

In the 1890s, the atmosphere was no less rough in Galena than it was in Joplin a few miles away. At this time, the two cities sprawled together, making a defined line between the two hard to identify as one went down the road. As in Joplin, the favorite pastime of miners in Galena was spending their paycheck in the saloons, gambling parlors and "bawdy" houses. The north portion of Main Street in Galena, which separated the city from Empire City to the north (which was known to be even rougher than Galena), was known as the Red Light Zone. With more than thirty thousand miners in town—most of whom were not from the area—it is not surprising that crime was rampant, and it was not unusual for an intoxicated miner to disappear after an argument at the bar, poker table, etc.

At this point in her life, Ma Staffleback, along with her sons Ed, George and Mike, was at heart an opportunist, and she set out to make money off of the miners. She opened a bordello at the corner of Main and Fort Streets in the Red Light Zone. The Staffleback bordello was very popular and a busy place, and Ma Staffleback became a wealthy woman in a short time.

Interior of one of the bedrooms in the Stefflebeck Bordello. This is reputed to be Ma Nance's room. *Courtesy of Paranormal Science Lab.*

Perhaps because of prior problems with the law, the Stafflebacks lived in a seemingly humble manner in an old log cabin nearby.

While there are variations in different accounts of the Stafflebacks' deeds in Galena, the following is the story generally told by local residents. One evening, Nance Staffleback was studying a miner, who was buying one drink after another, and noticed that he was paying for those drinks with gold coins kept in a leather pouch secured to his belt. Figuring from the size of the bag that it contained several hundred dollars, a cold, calculating plan formed in her mind. She waited until the man was very drunk and enticed him into one of the back rooms. Instead of the entertainment he had been expecting, the unfortunate man was greeted by one of the Staffleback sons, who attacked him with an ax, splitting the miner's head open. Later, the body was concealed in a canvas bag or feed sack and removed from the house under the cover of darkness in a buggy. The body was disposed of in one of the abandoned mine shafts in the area.

Ma Staffleback and her sons didn't stop with that murder, as their wicked deeds soon became more profitable than the bordello itself. Ma Staffleback's three sons and her boyfriend, Charles Wilson (who by some accounts was actually her husband by that point), assisted in the murders. Ma was careful to target miners who were transients with no ties to the area. In this way, it was less likely that someone would go searching for them after they went missing. She was also very prudent—she did not spend money extravagantly and, in fact, lived very frugally. She did not use banks, and she ran a cash business so no one had any idea how much money she had amassed. She avoided suspicion of the authorities, although records indicate that the police were very familiar with the bordello before accusations of murder surfaced. Estimates of the number of victims range between thirty and fifty, but it is unknown exactly how many men succumbed to Ma Nance's plot. Making the legend even more titillating is the rumor that Ma Staffleback buried her fortune made from the bordello and plundering the corpses of her murder victims, which is said to have been up to $50,000. Legend holds that the money is buried in or near the bordello. To this day, no trace of the buried treasure has been found.

Still, there are those who now proclaim that none of the murders were ax murders because Frank Galbraith, for whose murder the Stafflebacks were tried and convicted, was not killed with an ax. Ironically, Galbraith was not at the bordello as a client. He was, in fact, visiting the Staffleback home to call on Em Chapman, one of the Staffleback daughters, when an argument ensued. His murder was not planned or staged like those that occurred in

This staircase offers a glimpse of the fine detail in the Stefflebeck Bordello. *Courtesy of Paranormal Science Lab.*

the bordello, and as such, it is natural that the method of death would not necessarily be the same as the bordello murders. A known victim of foul play is more indicative of the bordello murder victim scenario. There were other men, mostly miners, who were known to have disappeared near the Staffleback house, but suspicion had not yet turned their way. One example was Matt McGuirk, who was found in an abandoned mine shaft near the Staffleback house and bordello four months before Frank Galbraith was killed. McGuirk's skull was bashed in and fractured in several places. This head trauma is consistent with the tales of ax murders at the bordello.

Some have claimed that the ax-murder story is a modern internet-era urban legend. However, there are published accounts supporting the notion that the Stafflebacks killed men with an ax. One such account was set out in William and Mabel Draper's *Old Grubstake Days in Joplin* in 1946:

> *The Stafflebacks made many strikes, but every time they struck, it was to kill a man. They were not miners; they were killers and robbers. Old Ma Staffleback kept a boardinghouse and a lot of pretty girls around her. They fed and entertained the miners with money—not only as a sporting house—more particularly, they ran a slaughterhouse. Their method was*

to get a man into the dining room, where he ate and drank with the girls, anticipating the good time to follow. While he was feeling good and a little dopey, one of the Staffleback boys would slip up behind him and strike him on the head with an ax. The girls would rob the corpse, after which the body would be thrown into one of the old mine shafts. Only one body was found which could be identified—Frank Galbraith. The bones of several others were discovered, but none could say how or when they met their fate. The Galena Sentinel, in a recent historical edition, said of the Staffleback gang: "From the portals of these places of sin, many a poor miner has been borne to his grave in some deserted shaft, and his disappearance was not remarked. Years afterward, perhaps, his bones were discovered, but there was nothing to tell his name or the story of his death. Although located in a state where law and order was generally observed, even at that date, the law was disregarded and officers were powerless to do their duty."

The murders may have gone on undetected for years longer but for a passerby spotting Galbraith's body floating in the abandoned shaft on July 19, 1897. Legend suggests that the murder was disclosed because of an argument Nancy had with her daughter-in-law Cora (married to George Staffleback), who, out of fear, claimed to have been a reluctant prostitute in the bordello. The legend states that Nancy and Cora had a heated exchange, reputedly because Cora was no longer willing to work as one of the girls in the bordello. Ma Nance threw Cora out of the house. In retaliation, Cora went to the police in town and informed them of the murders. This part of the Staffleback legend seems to have been a later embellishment, as the passerby reported the body to the police and not Cora, and her involvement in exposing the murder was less proactive than the legend suggests. As Larry Wood writes:

Authorities held an inquest, at which Marshall Parker and others testified that they had last seen Galbraith on a night about five weeks earlier in the company of an unknown man. Cherokee County deputy sheriff Charles Rains set out to locate the stranger and sent Constable Lafe Roe and Deputy Constable L.M. Radley to hunt down anyone who might remember hearing shots fired in the vicinity of the abandoned mine shaft near the suspected time of Galbraith's murder. Rain located Jesse Jacobs, who told the lawman of Galbraith's determination to visit the Stafflebac[k] house on the fateful night. Meanwhile, Rains' deputies inquired of numerous miners and finally located one who told them he had heard three shots near the Stafflebac[k] home, which was also near the abandoned shaft, on approximately the night in question. This confluence of circumstances cast immediate suspicion on the Stafflebac[k]s.

Upon inquiry, officers learned that Anna McCombs [by some accounts Ed Staffleback's common-law wife], Cora Stafflebac[k], and two other former residents of the Stafflebac[k] home had moved to nearby Joplin since the night of the murder. A party of lawmen went to Joplin on the evening of July 27 [1897] to interrogate the group. They found the sporting women at a "free and easy" in Joplin, and Deputy Rains extracted a confession from Anna McCombs and Cora Stafflebac[k], eyewitnesses to the murder. The pair told Rains that Ed Stafflebac[k] had done most of the work but that Old Lady Stafflebac[k], her son George, and Charles Wilson were also involved in the crime. The two women were not charged in the murder but were held as witnesses and taken back to Galena that night. Upon their return, the officers immediately set about rounding up the principals in the crime. They arrested Nancy Stafflebac[k] at her home and found Ed Stafflebac[k] on Main Street. Locating George Stafflebac[k] proved to be no problem, as he was already a guest of the county jail in Columbus for breaking into a boxcar a couple of weeks earlier. Charles Wilson was taken into custody the next day.

Police searched the bordello thoroughly but found no money taken from the victims. Searching nearby abandoned mine shafts, evidence of more than a dozen bodies were found, but none could be identified. The Staffleback saga has garnered other would-be revisionists with the passage of time—some even suggesting that there were no bordellos or brothels on north Main Street in Galena. Multiple contemporary reports reference a number of houses of ill fame as well as gambling parlors and other illegal pursuits in the vicinity. As to whether the Stafflebacks in particular ran a bordello, there are specific accounts, including testimony at the Galbraith murder trial. Additionally, another issue of speculation that has arisen in recent years is whether the attributed number of murders—thirty to fifty—is realistic. Accounts contemporaneous to the Galbraith murder trial suggest that circumstantial evidence from the number of missing miners in the area made the claims of thirty to fifty victims plausible. The *Kansas Semi-Weekly Capital* reported the events of the murder trial on September 17, 1897:

The trials of George and Edward Staffleback and Charles and Nancy Wilson for the murder of Frank Galbraith at Galena, Kansas, on the 19th day of last June have developed a carnival of crime only surpassed in the state by the famous Bender family. For several years, occasionally dead bodies would be found at the bottom of abandoned shafts which are to be found near at hand in any part of Galena or its suburbs, but the coroner's jury would usually have no suspicion of foul play, thinking perhaps that on some dark night, the deceased person had carelessly mistaken the road and walked into them, and the fall on the rocks at the bottom of the shaft accounted for not only the death but also for whatever wounds were found on the body. The defendants were all mutually interested in maintaining a house of ill-fame, and until this trial, it was supposed this was their only means of gaining a livelihood, and when it became necessary to replenish their harem if they could not entice some young victim into their clutches in any other manner, they would marry them. George had lately married a new wife [Cora], but as soon as she discovered what was expected of her, she skipped out to her old home. When George found that she would not return under such circumstances, he wrote pledging that if she would return to him that they would live separate and apart from the other Stafflebacks. This induced her to return.

George at once began his efforts to persuade her to embark in a career of infamy. She refused but did not dare to leave, for she had seen enough of the gang to be afraid to directly oppose them, but she was only awaiting her time. After she had been at the Stafflebacks about ten or twelve days, murder occurred. Last summer, there was first seen at the Stafflebacks' two very handsome and attractive young girls supposed to be about 15 and 17 years of age. Those visiting the house could never learn any particulars about them, either how they came there, where they came from or what their names were. After being there about three or four months, they suddenly disappeared. Cora Staffleback…now states on oath as a witness in the Galbraith case that both girls were cruelly murdered. She says that Ed Staffleback killed one of them by crushing her skull with the butt end of a revolver and that his brother Mike then seized the other girl and beat her brains out by pounding her head on the floor. Both bodies, Mrs. Staffleback declares, were rolled under a bed until night, when they were carried out and thrown into an abandoned shaft. Last summer, a man by the name of Frank Smith, of Galena, mysteriously disappeared, and Cora says he is another victim of the Stafflebacks. Three years ago, a citizen of Joplin, Mo., by the name of Moorehead was found in a shaft—another alleged Staffleback victim. They have escaped so long that they became careless. In listening to the evidence, the entire family seems the most unconcerned persons in the courtroom, frequently laughing at blunders of the witnesses.

The tale of the two young nameless girls is reminiscent of the Galbraith murder in that they were personal in nature and not set up for robbery in the bordello. Cora testified that Ed and Mike, then in their late twenties/early thirties, would "follow circuses and fairs with various 'fakes'," where they met and induced the teenage girls to return to Galena with them. She further testified that the girls were not inmates in the bordello for other men's pleasures but were there to show affection only for Ed and Mike. On the night of the girls' murders, Ed found his girl sitting on another man's lap. He ordered the man to leave, and afterwards, an argument with the girl ensued, leading him to pistol whip her and bludgeon her to death. Mike then killed his girl so she would not have an opportunity to tell anyone what Ed had done to her friend.

It is unknown exactly what motivated George Staffleback to confess on the witness stand at his own trial, but his testimony was as damaging as his wife's. George had not been in the courtroom for Cora's testimony, but his confession on the stand was similar in detail to her testimony. In particular, he related the events of Galbraith's murder and further testified that Galbraith was not the only victim. He stated that about two years earlier, they had slain an Italian peddler and robbed him before disposing of his body in the same mine shaft in which Frank Galbraith was found.

The sensational facts surrounding the trial of the Stafflebacks were reported across the nation, adding to the legend that grew around the bordello and the rumored buried fortune. The September 25, 1897 edition of the Utica, New York *Saturday Globe* reported the facts of the crimes in detail while exaggerating others:

> *Their Trade Was Crime: From Petty Thievery to Most Horrible Butchery: This Infamous Family Ran the Gamut and Now Two are Under Sentence of Death, While the Mother is Guilty of Murder*
>
> *Galena, Kan. Sept. 16.*
>
> *There may have been more wicked families in Sodom and Gomorrah of old than the Staffleback family of this place, three of whose members have recently been found guilty of murder, but it may be doubted if a more loathsome set of people ever before existed on this continent, either in a state of civilization or savagery, than the moral monsters the Stafflebacks, who have trafficked in every crime and vice from thievery to butchery, and two of whom, at least, will soon end their lives on the scaffold. George and Ed*

Staffleback have been found guilty of murder in the first degree and unless lynched will be legally executed, while the mother—hoary in crime as in years, she is now 66—has been found guilty of murder in the second degree and will end her years in prison.

Nancy Staffleback had led a most remarkable career of crime and has trained her progeny to follow in her footsteps. Of her 13 children, not one has led an upright life, and not one has a trait of character to redeem even in part, the general coarseness and criminality of their natures. She was born in Alleghany County, N.Y. Her maiden name was Chase, and her early years were spent in Wisconsin. Through her mother, she inherited a strain of Wyandotte Indian blood, and perhaps this may have had something to do with the natural viciousness of her character. When young, she married a Swiss, Michael Staffleback, in Dubuque, Ia. After some changes, they moved to Lawrence County, Mo., where they settled on a farm. Here they quarreled. The husband was charged by his wife and some of his children with unmentionable crimes, and the husband accused the wife of crimes equally revolting to both moral and natural laws. The result was that the husband left the neighborhood and has not since been heard from. The airing of their family differences in court had the effect of making Lawrence County too hot for Nancy, and her brood and they moved to a place known as Swindle Hill, in the town of Joplin, Jasper County. It was a fit abode for such characters. Here congregated the degraded of both sexes, women who had forgotten the meaning of decency and men who were practiced in every crime. A man's life was not safe in the place after dark, and policemen never ventured into it singly. Here the Stafflebacks lived several years, the sons practicing thievery and other crimes, for which some of them received sentences in jail, and the girls consorting with the degraded of both sexes.

They committed one murder, at least, here, but the story of this will come later. Ultimately, the vile den of the Stafflebacks was raided, and two of the sons were sent to the penitentiary.

Three years ago, the family moved to "Picker's Point," an unsavory place on the outskirts of this city. They took up their abode in a long-deserted shanty within a few rods of which were a number of deserted shafts, where some time or other men had prospected for lead or zinc. The place is a hotbed for crime. Scattered around are miserable hovels, the homes of depraved women and men. Here vice reaches a depth that decency dare not attempt to describe. Rough miners, many of them foreigners, frequent the hovels and gamble and drink and swear. Ribald revelry is often interrupted by a fight that ends in murder. Then the shafts, the silent yawning pits of the ground, are charged with another victim, which they receive into their dark depths never to yield again. If these shafts were today made to give up their ghastly tenants—fully 50 undiscovered murders would be revealed.

Amid such congenial surroundings, the Staffleback family resumed their career of crime. At this time, the family consisted of Mother Nance, Ed, George, Mike, Cora, Louise and Emma. All these were children of the old woman except Cora, who was married to George. The latter and Ed had a short time before been released from the penitentiary and had joined the family at "Picker's Point." And now another man, Charles Wilson, who passed as a husband of Nancy, drifted into the gang. Two girls, Rose Bayne and Anna McCombs, also took up their abode with the Staffleback family. In their different ways, these people led their criminal lives with Mother Nance acting as the evil genius of the gang. Time and again, the den in which they lived was raided, and one or more was arrested for some petty offense. But the gang took this as a matter of course.

Last June, however, occurred an event that brought the Stafflebacks to grief. This was the murder of a miner, Frank Galbraith. He had gone to the Staffleback house on invitation from Emma, but the old woman refused him admittance. He returned, and then a row began. This is the story of it as given by Anna McCombs, who witnessed the affair:

"I heard the row begin and stepped outside and around the corner of the log hut. The old woman grabbed her corn knife and ran Galbraith out of the house. Then Wilson and Ed got their guns and began shooting at Galbraith, who started to run down the road. Wilson fired first but missed. Then Ed fired, and I could tell that he hit him, for Frank put his hand to his hip and fell. But he got right up again and ran on. He couldn't run very fast, and Ed ran alongside of him, put his gun to his head and fired. Frank threw his hand up to his head and fell by the side of the road. Ed took the knife from the old woman and started to finish Frank by cutting his throat. All this time, me and Cora had been running along after them. I grabbled Ed by the arm and begged him not to do it. 'Let me alone or I'll slit your throat,' he said. Then he turned and slit Galbraith's throat. The blood spurted out. The old woman took the knife and wiped it on her apron."

"I felt sick, and me and Cora laid down in the weeds so we could see them and they couldn't see us. They thought we had gone to the house. I was afraid to look until Cora whispered, 'They're pulling his clothes off.' Then I looked…Ed took him by the shoulders and George took one *leg and Wilson the other. They carried him to the old shaft and threw him in."*

A month after, the body of Galbraith was seen floating at the bottom of the shaft, and an investigation into the crime was started. Ed, George and Nancy Staffleback were arrested, tried and convicted of the murder, and an effort was made to apprehend Wilson, who was also implicated in the killing. Wilson, however, had fled and the authorities are now searching for him.

The arrest of the Stafflebacks led to other horrible disclosures. Released from the fear in which they had lived by the Stafflebacks, Cora Staffleback and Rose Bayne told their stories of further murders committed by the hell-influenced family. Two years ago, two girls took up their abode in the Staffleback house. One night, in a fit of passion, Mike Staffleback beat one of them into insensibility and finally death, and lest the other girl should tell of the affair, she was beaten to death by Ed Staffleback. The brothers then wrapped the bodies in sheets and threw them down an abandoned shaft.

A short time afterward, the brothers, Mike, Ed and George, attacked and killed a peddler who was stopping overnight at the house and divided his money.

Another murder of which members of the Staffleback family are guilty was that of an old man named Rosenbaugh. Ed, Mike and a man named Billy Martin made way with him while the Stafflebacks were living in Joplin. He was killed for $85 in pension money which he was known to have on his person.

Still another murder the Stafflebacks are believed to have committed while in Joplin is that of a man named Moorhouse. Moorhouse mysteriously disappeared while there, and from conversations held between the Stafflebacks, Cora Staffleback is of the opinion that the man was murdered.

The latest phase in the Staffleback matter was the burning during the week by a crowd of citizens of the Staffleback den. A search for more bodies in the old abandoned shafts will be immediately begun by the county authorities.

Many of the facts cited in the foregoing newspaper account, including the belief that the Stafflebacks were responsible for a large number of unsolved murders, are mirrored in other contemporary reports. The *Kansas Semi-Weekly Capital* reported, "There are yet other parties unaccounted for which Mrs. Stevens, the prosecutor, says will be enrolled among the Staffleback dead. In fact, there is no telling where the list will end."

The testimony of Cora Staffleback revealed the extent of the murder spree and inflamed passions of the town against the Stafflebacks with details such as that after throwing Frank Galbraith's body into the mine shaft, Nancy went back to the house and calmly cooked a pot of chili for everyone. Crowds of up to five hundred gathered to watch the hoist dredge the bottom of the mine shafts near the Staffleback house and bordello. Cora was brought from Columbus by the sheriff to watch the operation. The first of the grizzly discoveries was brought to light in the September 16, 1897 edition of the *Dallas Morning News*:

> *A large crowd surrounds the mouth of the pit at all times, and great interest is shown in each bucketful of dirt which comes to the surface. This interest was rewarded about 9 o'clock this morning by the appearance of a wooden club on which was a bunch of hair. This was carefully examined by barbers and others and pronounced human. It is said on the streets that a company of vigilantes has been organized to go to Columbus in case bodies are found and lynch the entire Staffleback family. It is said that the man who will lead the crowd is the one who commanded at the lynching of Joe Thornton in Joplin ten years or more ago. This committee of forty-five is said to be mostly workingmen, but a number of merchants have signified their approval of the scheme and their willingness to join in the work. If the crowd should go to Columbus and be successful in gaining access to the jail, the Stafflebacks will not be the only ones hanged, as there are nine men in that structure who have been recently convicted of murder in the first degree. If nothing is found in this shaft, another one nearly 100 feet deep will be searched. This is the shaft out of which some bloody clothing was taken Tuesday.*

The recovery of bloody clothing with "particles of flesh adhering thereto," a wooden cub with a "bunch" of human hair on it, bones and a "part of a woman's waist" over several days signaled the last straw for the local permanent residents, who were tired of the criminal element brought into town by the miners. The *Topeka Weekly Capital* reported, "The people of Galena are thoroughly aroused. A number of murders have been committed here lately, and many disreputable characters have come here from other places. There is likely to be a determined effort to clear the moral atmosphere by making the town too hot to hold those not wanted."

It is known that the Stafflebacks lived in a log house separate from the bordello and that the log house was torched by a vigilante mob of about

The view facing north past the Stefflebeck Bordello toward Empire City. In the 1890s, this stretch of road was lined with bawdy houses and gambling parlors. *Courtesy of Paranormal Science Lab.*

forty men on September 16, 1897. The alarm was not sounded until the house was almost entirely burnt to the ground, and when notified, the fire department made no effort to extinguish the fire. The bordello, however, was not torched. It was at this point that Ed Staffleback went "stark raving mad" out of fear of being lynched and was restrained in a straitjacket in the county jail.

October 1, 1897, was sentencing day for the defendants in the Galbraith murder case, which included the largest number of defendants sentenced in one case to that date in Kansas. George Staffleback was sentenced to hang but would end up serving a life sentence. Nancy Staffleback was sentenced to serve twenty-one years, and Charles Wilson twenty-five years. Mike Staffleback was sentenced to serve seven years on larceny charges related to the robbery of Galbraith's corpse. Ed Staffleback's fate was potentially complicated by his recent display of mental incapacity. The *Kansas City Journal* reported the legal maneuvering on October 2, 1897:

> *In the case of Ed Staffleback, his attorney procured a writ of habeas corpus and had him before Probate Judge Sapp to test his sanity. He had*

117

been convicted of murder in the first degree, and before Judge Skidmore would sentence him, he called in three physicians to obtain their opinion upon the question of sanity of the prisoner. Their decision was that he was insane. There is a rumor that Judge Skidmore will decide that he is sane, in which event he will be sentenced tomorrow to be hanged and will be sent to Lansing with the other prisoners.

The rumor was correct. Judge Skidmore found that Ed Staffleback was sane and therefore could be sentenced. He was sentenced to life in prison. The defendants were sent to the Kansas state prison in Lansing and then transferred to the state prison at Leavenworth. Ed Staffleback died in prison at Leavenworth in 1905 due to unknown circumstances.

The arched window, now boarded up, was actually a walkway for "the girls" to stand and entice miners into the bordello. *Courtesy of Paranormal Science Lab.*

Cora Staffleback and Anna McCombs faded from the public eye after the trial, and it is unknown what happened to them. The story that the father, Michael Staffleback, left his family when they were living in Lawrence County is incorrect, as he was in the household in Joplin. Although he left the family in 1895, he did not wander far. He died at the age of eighty-one on May 15, 1899, in Joplin. Just as he had attempted to keep his name separate from that of his son Mike regarding his criminal activities in Lawrence County, in death, the press extended the same courtesy to the father. The May 16, 1899 edition of the *Kansas City Journal* noted:

Michael Staffleback Dead: He Was Honest Himself, But He Had a Lot of Murderous Kin

Joplin, Mo., May 15—Michael Staffleback, the former husband of the old murderess, Madam Staffleback, and father of the Staffleback boys, died here today of cancer of the stomach. He was an honest old man and had had nothing to do with his former wife and sons for several years past.

Nancy Staffleback, who called herself Nancy Wilson by this time, died from pneumonia on March 9, 1909, at the age of seventy-nine in Leavenworth Prison having never revealed any details of the murders or of the buried treasure. Nancy asked to be allowed to die outside of prison, but this requested was denied. Her son George and husband, Charles Wilson, were allowed to join her. Mike already had been released but was then serving a term in the Missouri penitentiary on theft-related charges. George pleaded with prison officials to allow his mother to die outside of prison but was told that they had no power to do so. The *Leavenworth Times* reported on March 10, 1909:

The death of Mrs. Staffleback was intensely pathetic and caused much commotion in the female ward of the penitentiary. It is seldom that a woman dies in the female ward, and when it was announced this morning that she could not live, the other 33 female prisoners acted as though they were about to sustain the loss of a near relative.

Nancy Staffleback ultimately made her way back to Missouri and Route 66, as her body was sent to Joplin, where her youngest daughter, Mary Kenyon, took charge of it. After her death, treasure hunters flocked to Galena upon publication of the story, some coming from as far away as Colorado. The bordello was ransacked and floorboards pried up but again no stash of money was found. To this day, it is unknown where the money was hidden, whether in the bordello or somewhere else in the Galena area, or exactly how much was hidden. Likewise, it is unknown if one of her family members or some other person with knowledge of the murders, perhaps another one of the girls working at the bordello, quietly took upon themselves the chore of safekeeping the money.

Charles Wilson seems lost to history as to his fate after Nancy's death. Michael was released from the penitentiary in 1905 and lived a long life, perhaps attempting to avoid connection to the infamous murders in Galena, Kansas. He died in Poplar Bluff, Missouri, some three hundred miles east of Galena, on September 2, 1944, at the age of seventy-six. His occupation was listed as a farmer, and the cause of death was listed as injuries from an accident. The interesting thing is that his name on his death certificate is spelled Mickel Staffleback. However, the birth date is correct, and his parents were listed as Mickel Staffleback, of Germany, and Nancy Chase. Although his father was named Michael and from Switzerland, the small changes may well have been motivated out of a desire for anonymity. He was listed as divorced twice and a widower. His third wife, Alice, had died on June 2, 1940, of kidney disease.

Regardless of the fate of the stolen money, the bordello has stood empty for decades, occupied at various times only to be vacated once more. It now stands boarded up. The old house has lost the luster of its former glory and sits slowly rotting away, holding secrets just as Ma Stefflebeck did. Recently, new owners purchased the property and plan to restore the bordello to its former glory and reopen it as a bed and breakfast inn.

As if the Staffleback bordello needed more of a macabre element, it has long been said that the ghosts of the Stafflebacks' victims have remained at

Lisa Livingston-Martin in front of the Stefflebeck Bordello. *Courtesy of Paranormal Science Lab.*

the bordello all these years. I have spoken with people who lived in the house at times or served as caretakers, and they tell tales of a foreboding, haunted house in which the ghosts make themselves well known to the living. As part of Paranormal Science Lab, I've had the opportunity to investigate the old bordello multiple times, and the old Victorian lady lived up to her haunted reputation. Among the unexplained phenomena were electronic voice phenomena (voices recorded on audio devices that were not heard at the time of recording) of multiple voices, including a gruff man's voice saying, "Nance," which Nancy was often called. In one bedroom, an investigator asked, "Why are you here?" and a man is heard on audio replying, "He killed me." In another room, the question was asked, "Did anyone die here?" and a different voice responds, "Must have died." Balls of light were captured on video, and a chilling photo of what resembles a tortured, elongated face was documented. For those wishing to stay at a very wicked bed and breakfast inn, I highly recommend that you watch for the Galena Murder Bordello to open its doors to the public.

Bibliography

Barrett, Paul W., and Mary H. Barrett. *Young Brothers Massacre*. Columbia: University of Missouri Press, 1988.

Belk, Colleen. *Jasper County, Missouri Tombstones and Civil War Data*. Huntsville, AR: Century Enterprises, 1990.

Bourbon News. "Notorious Stafflebacks Sentenced." October 5, 1897.

Bunker, Edward. *Education of a Felon: A Memoir*. New York: St. Martin's Press, 2001.

Carmack, Gary. "Paramedic's Corner: Reviewing the 1968 Soto Club Murders." *Waynesville Daily Guide*. http://www.waynesvilledailyguide. com/article/20081015/NEWS/310159905.

Carthage Patriot. "Is Jesse James Dead? That Is the All-Consuming Question, The *Patriot* Believes That He Was Shot If Not Killed, The Latest News from Joplin Concerning the Affair." November 6, 1879.

———. "Jesse James, Reported Killing of This Noted Outlaw." November 6, 1879.

The Chieftan. June 21, 1894.

———. August 2, 1894.

Cottrell, Steve. *Haunted Ozarks Battlefields: Civil War Ghost Stories and Brief Battle Histories*. Gretna, LA: Pelican Publishing Co., 2010.

Curtis, C.H. Skip. *Birthplace of Route 66: Springfield, MO*. Springfield, MO: Curtis Enterprises, 2001.

Dallas Morning News. "Find Bunch of Hair: First Reward in Search for Staffleback Victims, Galena All Wrought Up Over the Probable Find of the Bodies—Columbus Jail Very Insecure." September 16, 1897.

Draper, William, and Mabel Draper. *Old Grubstake Days in Joplin*. Girard, KS: Haldeman-Julius Publications, 1946.

Dresbold, Michelle, and James Kwalwasser. *Sex, Lies and Handwriting: A Top Expert Reveals the Secrets Hidden in Your Handwriting*. New York: Free Press, 2008.

Ensminger, Richard A. "Quantrill's Guerillas: Members in the Civil War." Kansas Heritage Group, http://www.kansasheritage.org/research/quantrill.html.

Evening Hour. "Old Nancy's Brood: Terrible Crimes of the Staffleback Family: The Benders Are Outbendered, Evidence Secured of Six Murders and Possibility that a Total of Fifty May Be Ascribed to the Inmates of the Galena Den." September 23, 1897.

Gilbert, Joan. *Missouri Ghosts: Spirits, Haunts and Related Lore*. Columbia, MO: Pebble Publishing, 1997.

Gilmore, John: *L.A. Despair: A Landscape of Crimes and Bad Times*. Los Angeles: Amok Books, 2005.

Goodrich, Thomas. *Black Flag: Guerrilla Warfare on the Western Border, 1861–1865: A Riveting Account of a Bloody Chapter in Civil War History*. Bloomington: Indiana University Press, 1999.

Goodspeed Publishing Co. *History of Laclede, Camden, Dallas, Webster, Wright, Texas, Pulaski, Phelps and Dent Counties, Missouri*. Indexed Edition. Chicago, Goodspeed Publishing Co., 1889.

Grahame-Smith, Seth. *Abraham Lincoln: Vampire Hunter*. New York: Grand Central Publishing, 2010.

Greer, Lillie Johnson. *Through the Years: A History of Peace Church Cemetery (104 Years) and Sherwood Cemetery (100 Years) in Galena Township*. N.p., 1961.

Harper, Kimberly. *White Man's Heaven: The Lynching and Expulsion of Blacks in the Southern Ozarks, 1894–1909*. Fayetteville: University of Arkansas Press, 2010.

Hinds, Bob. *Ozark Pioneers: Their Trials and Triumphs*. Willow Springs, MO: Bob Hinds Books, 2002.

Joplin Daily Herald. "The James Brothers, George Shepherd Says He Shot and Killed One of Them." November 4, 1879.

Joplin Globe. "Effort Under Way to Save Notorious Galena Bordello." August 17, 2012.

———. November 29, 1978.

Kansas City Journal. "For the Galbraith Murder, Five Men and Three Women Arrested at Galena, Kas. and Taken to Columbus." July 29, 1987.

———. "Michael Staffleback Dead: He Was Honest Himself, but He Had a Lot of Murderous Kin." May 16, 1899.

———. "Stafflebacks Sentenced." October 2, 1897.

Kansas Semi-Weekly Capital. "Galena's Benders: Startling Developments in the Galbraith Murder Trial." September 17, 1897.

Krajicek, David J. *True Crime: Missouri: The State's Most Notorious Criminal Cases.* Mechanicsville, PA: Stackpole Books, 2011.

Leavenworth Times. March 9, 1909.

Livingston, Joel T. *A History of Jasper County, Missouri, and Its People.* Chicago: Lewis Publishing Co., 1912.

Livingston, John C., Jr. *Such a Foe as Livingston: The Campaign of Conferedate Major Thomas R. Livingston's First Missouri Cavalry Battalion of Southwest Missouri.* Wyandotte, OK: Gregath Publishing Company, 2004.

Lloyd and Bauman Publishers. *The Mineral Wealth of Southwest Missouri.* Joplin, MO: Lloyd and Bauman Publishers, 1874.

Long, John Wilson. *Stanford University School of Medicine and the Predecessor Schools: An Historical Perspective.* Stanford, CA: Stanford University, 1998.

McCord, William M. *The Psychopath and Milieu Therapy.* New York: Academic Press, 1982.

McCord, William M., and Joan McCord. *Psychopathy and Delinquency.* New York: Grune and Stratton, 1956.

Monks, William. *A History of Southern Missouri and Northern Arkansas.* West Plains, MO: West Plains Journal Co., 1907.

Morgan, R.D. *Irish O'Malley and the Ozark Mountain Boys.* Stillwater, OK: New Forums Press, 2011.

Morning Times. "A Revelation of Depravity; Members of the Staffleback Family Confess Many Crimes." September 15, 1897.

Musick, John R. *Stories of Missouri.* New York: American Book Company, 1897.

National Register of Historic Places. Bonnie and Clyde Garage Apartment, Joplin, Newton County, Missouri, National Register #09000302.

New York Times. "The Galena Murder Mystery." September 17, 1897.

———. "Pixar's 'Cars' Got Its Kicks on Route 66." May 21, 2006.

Offutt, Jason. *Haunted Missouri: A Ghostly Guide to the Show-Me State's Most Spirited Spots.* Kirksville, MO: Truman State University Press, 2007.

Orlet, Christopher. "The Thrill Kill Cult." *American Spectator.* February 16, 2012.

Randolph, Vance. *Ozark Ghost Stories: Gruesome and Humorous Tales of the Supernatural in the Backwoods of the South.* Photo-facsimile edition of the 1944 Haldeman-Julius Publications edition. Forrest City, AR: Marshall Vance, 1982.

———. *Ozark Magic and Folklore.* New York: Dover Publications, 1964.

Riordan, Timothy B. *Prince of Quacks: The Notorious Life of Dr. Francis Tumblety, Charlatan and Jack the Ripper Suspect.* Jefferson, NC: McFarland & Company, Inc., 2009.

Rutter, Michael. *Bedside Book of Bad Girls: Outlaw Women of the American West.* Helena, MT: Farcountry Press, 2008.

Salem Review Press. "Like the Benders: Many Crimes Laid at the Door of the Staffleback Family." September 17, 1897.

Schrantz, Ward L. *Jasper County, Missouri, in the Civil War.* Reprint. Carthage, MO: Carthage, Missouri Kiwanis Club, 2010.

Shaner, Dolph. *The Story of Joplin.* New York: Stratford House, Inc., 1948.

Shepley, Carol Ferring. "The Lemp Family of St. Louis: Successful Beginnings and Tragic Endings." *Voices.* Missouri History Museum Press, 2008.

———. *Movers and Shakers, Scalawags and Suffragettes: Tales from Bellefontaine Cemetery.* St. Louis: Missouri History Museum Press, 2008.

Shoemaker, Floyd Calvin. *Missouri and Missourians: Land of Contrasts and People of Achievements, Vol. One.* Chicago: Lewis Publishing Co., 1943.

Simpson, Leslie. *Postcard History Series: Joplin.* Charleston, SC: Arcadia Publishing, 2011.

Springfield Leader and Press. "Outlaws Take Two Men as Prisoners; Kidnap Men on Wild Ride Through Ozarks and Gun Battle with Officers; Woman With Bandits, Bonnie Parker Laughs Gleefully as Bullets are Rained on Possemen." February 13, 1934.

———. "Thomas A. Persell." January 27, 1933.

Springfield News-Leader. "Bank Robbers Bonnie, Clyde Kidnapped Policeman in 1933." October 10, 1999.

Steele, Phillip W., and Steve Cottrell. *Civil War in the Ozarks.* Gretna, LA: Pelican Publishing Co., 2003.

Stephens, Ann S. *Pictorial History of the War for the Union.* Cincinnati, OH: James R. Hawley, 1863.

Stevens, Walter Barlow. *Missouri, the Center State: 1821–1915.* Chicago: S.J. Clarke Publishing Co., 1915.

Time. "Sequels: Billy's Last Words." December 22, 1952.

Topeka Weekly Capital. September 17, 1897.

Tremeear, Janice. *Missouri's Haunted Route 66: Ghosts Along the Mother Road.* Charleston, SC: The History Press, 2010.

Tumblety, Francis. *A Few Passages in the Life of Dr. Francis Tumblety.* Cincinnati, OH: Self published, 1866.

———. *A Sketch of the Life of Francis Tumblety: Presenting an Outline of His Wonderful Career as a Physician.* New York: N.p., 1893.

Twain, Mark. *The Adventures of Tom Sawyer.* Hartford, CN: American Publishing Company, 1899.

———. *Life on the Mississippi.* New York: Harper and Brothers, 1901.

Utica Saturday Globe. "Their Trade Was Crime: From Petty Thievery to Most Horrible Butchery." September 25, 1897.

VanGilder, Marvin L. *Jasper County: The First Two Hundred Years.* Rich Hill, MO: Bell Books, 1995.

Van Ravenswaay, Charles. *St. Louis: An Informal History of the City and Its People, 1764–1865.* Jefferson City: Missouri Historical Society Press, 1991.

Wallis, Michael, and Suzanne Fitzgerald Wallis. *The Art of Cars.* San Francisco: Chronicle Books, 2006.

Washington University School of Medicine. "Institutional Roots, 1840–1908." http://beckerexhibits.wustl.edu/wusm-hist/roots/index.htm.

Weiser, Kathy. "Kansas Legends: A Murderous Tale of Scandal and Treasure in Galena." Legends of America, www.legendsofamerica.com/ks-galenatreasure.html.

Wood, Larry. *The Civil War on the Lower Kansas–Missouri Border.* Joplin, MO: Hickory Press, 2003.

———. *Other Noted Guerillas of the Civil War in Missouri.* Joplin, MO: Hickory Press, 2007.

———. *Ozarks Gunfights and Other Notorious Incidents.* Gretna, LA: Pelican Publishing, 2010.

WEBSITES

Community in Conflict: http://www.ozarkscivilwar.org/
Historic Joplin: http://www.historicjoplin.org/
Joplin Missouri Public Library: http://www.joplinpubliclibrary.org/
Mark Twain Cave: www.marktwaincave.com/
Missouri Digital Heritage Collection: http://www.sos.mo.gov/mdh/
Paranormal Science Lab: www.paranormalsciencelab.com
St. Louis Historic Preservation. http://stlcin.missouri.org/history/index.cfm

About the Author

A lifelong resident of Missouri, Lisa Livingston-Martin lives with her children in Webb City. Lisa has practiced law in southwest Missouri for more than twenty years and has long-standing interests in history and the paranormal. She is a co–team leader of Paranormal Science Lab (www.paranormalsciencelab. com), a research group that focuses on paranormal research at historic locations. Lisa is

Lisa Livingston-Martin. *Courtesy of Paranormal Science Lab.*

a frequent speaker on the paranormal and the connection between the history of locations and paranormal activity. She graduated from Missouri State University with a BS in political science, later obtaining a JD from Washington University in St. Louis Law School. Lisa is the author of *Civil War Ghosts of Southwest Missouri* and *Haunted Joplin*, also published by The History Press.